BRAZILIAN JIU-JITSU BASICS

MASTERING THE ESSENTIAL TECHNIQUES

GENE SIMCO

D1601765

CITADEL PRESS
Kensington Publishing Corp.
www.kensingtonbooks.com

WARNING

The techniques presented in this book are dangerous. Before you begin your Brazilian Jiu-jitsu training, you should consult a physician. You and your partner should always communicate with each other and stop when the other signals. All techniques should be practiced under the supervision of a qualified instructor. The author of this book shall not be held liable for the misuse of any information contained within.

CITADEL PRESS BOOKS are published by

Kensington Publishing Corp.
850 Third Avenue
New York, NY 10022

Copyright © 2004 Gene Simco

All Kensington titles, imprints, and distributed lines are available at special quantity discounts for bulk purchases for sales promotions, premiums, fund-raising, educational, or institutional use. Special book excerpts or customized printings can also be created to fit specific needs. For details, write or phone the office of the Kensington special sales manager: Kensington Publishing Corp., 850 Third Avenue, New York, NY 10022, attn: Special Sales Department; phone 1-800-221-2647

CITADEL PRESS and the Citadel logo are Reg. U.S. Pat. & TM Off.

First printing: January 2004

10 9 8 7 6 5 4 3 2 1

Printed in the United States of America

Cataloging data may be obtained from the Library of Congress

ISBN 0-8065-2663-7

Editing - Heather Simco
Photography - Chris Lavine, Adam Weismann
Modeling - Gene Simco, Bob Burlingame, Christina McLaughlin, Stephan Duvivier, Neel Choudhury, Sarah Testerman, Rob Constance
Design and Layout - Chris Lavine, Gene Simco

Table of Contents

INTRODUCTION

This purpose of this book is to provide students of Brazilian Jiu-jitsu who are at a beginner level with detailed descriptions of the art's basic techniques. This book is not a replacement for a qualified instructor. This book was written as a literary prerequisite to **Brazilian Jiu-jitsu, The Master Text**; once you have a practical understanding of the techniques in this book, I highly recommend acquiring The Master Text. Some techniques have been taken directly from the Master Text and given more thorough explanations, geared for beginners. This will also answer the frequently asked question: what techniques from the Master Text do I work on first?

At this level, a student's focus should be on the basic body positioning and fundamental concepts of the art. I have not gone into depth about the specific rules and guidelines of sport Jiu-jitsu practice, as it is more important at this level to learn the techniques of Jiu-jitsu unbound by sport specific strategy. It is important to keep in mind as you read this book; you understand the following techniques described within are the fundamental techniques of Jiu-jitsu. You will carry these fundamentals with you during your practice at both a beginner and advanced level of the art. Therefore, these move-

ments are not only to be used by beginners, but are techniques beginners must learn that will create a foundation on which other techniques will be placed. I have been careful not to include too many techniques because at this level, a lower number of techniques at higher proficiency is more important than "knowing" a bunch of moves that you can't actually do when it counts.

The study and practice of Brazilian Jiu-jitsu has improved my life in ways that few words can accurately describe. It is my greatest hope that with this book as a guide, Brazilian Jiu-jitsu will improve your life as it did mine.

Thank You for your Patronage and Support!

Sincerely,
Gene "Aranha" Simco

What is Jiu-jitsu?

Jiu-jitsu is a complete art of self-defense whose techniques are deeply rooted in the form of ancient wrestling movements. The practice of Jiu-jitsu has two basic forms: the learning of each movement through drilling and practice with no resistance between participants, and sport. Sport will allow two students of the art to practice realistically with resistance while providing a balance of reality and safety through a set of guidelines and rules that each participant must agree to and follow.

Jiu-jitsu by definition, means "gentle art". The basic concept is that a practitioner of the art is looking for the least harmful way to stop or restrain an attacker and protect him from harm. For this, a Jiu-jitsu practitioner will most commonly apply submission holds to immobilize an attacker. Because of this "gentle" method of technical application, students of the art may engage in its practice more frequently and at a much older age than other martial arts.

Jiu-jitsu is an art of positional dominance; this simply means that during an altercation, a practitioner of Jiu-jitsu will attempt to position his body in a way that will make him less vulnerable to a harmful attack. In doing so, this body positioning will create opportunities for a Jiu-jitsu practitioner to attack or counter-attack and subdue his assailant.

In accordance with the philosophy of Jiu-jitsu, the techniques of this text are organized by position. Each position is explained, as simply yet thoroughly as possible, then fundamental submission and restraining techniques that may be applied from that position will be detailed.

Brief History of Jiu-jitsu

Jiu-jitsu is said to have originated in India thousands of years ago as a form of wrestling. From India these 'wrestling' techniques traveled to China, then to Japan, where they became systemized. This system became known as Yawara and was not known as Jiu-jitsu until the sixteenth century. Jiu-jitsu, meaning 'gentle art', became widely practiced in Japan as the Samurai's art where it was refined into the deadliest of all martial arts on the battlefield.

Eventually, in Japan many variations of the art (Jiu-jitsu) took shape, including Karate, Aikido, and Judo. But these arts were missing essential pieces of what the complete art of Jiu-jitsu originally held. Soon the sun had set on the day of the once mighty Samurai; the gun had replaced the sword and new sportive ways to practice martial arts were developed. This lack of 'reality' created years of confusion in the martial arts community, a confusion that legendary Bruce Lee would later refer to as the 'classical mess'.

The 'sport arts', such as Judo and Kendo were wonderful in the way of offering it's practitioners a safe way to realistically train the techniques of their system, but often limited it's practitioners with too many rules to maintain it's effectiveness as a combative style. The more traditional 'combat' schools were simply practicing techniques no longer suitable for modern day combat, and with no way to safely test them, practicing these arts became like swimming without water.

It wasn't until the sport art of Judo, born of the combat techniques of Jiu-jitsu were introduced to the Gracie family in Brazil that the art of Jiu-jitsu would be brought to life again. Judo was introduced to the Gracie family in Brazil (1914) by Esai Maeda who was also known as Conde Koma. Maeda was a champion of Judo and a direct student of its founder, Jigoro Kano at the Kodokan in Japan. He was born in 1878, and became a student of Judo in 1897. In 1904 Maeda was given the opportunity to travel to the United States with one of his teachers, Tsunejiro Tomita. While in the U.S. they would demonstrate the art of Judo for Teddy Roosevelt at the White House, and cadets at the West Point Military Academy. Maeda would eventually part ways with Tomita, and settle in Brazil. Maeda was staying in Sao Palo City to help establish a Japanese Immigration colony. At this time Brazil held the largest population of Japanese people outside Japan. He was aided in Brazil by Gastao Gracie, a Brazilian of Scottish decent, who's first experience with Jiu-jitsu was most likely through managing an Italian boxer named Alfredi Leconti, who fought a friend of Maeda in November of 1916.

To show gratitude to Gracie for his help in the colonization, Maeda taught Gastao's son Carlos the basic techniques of Jiu-jitsu. Carlos Gracie then taught his brothers Oswaldo, Jorge, Gastao, and Helio. This was the birth of Brazilian Jiu-jitsu.

Finding a School

It is important to find the right school. This will determine the rest of your Jiu-jitsu 'career'. Once you have searched locally through the Internet and yellow pages, you must decide which school is right for you. Your first concern should be the legitimacy of the school's instructor. To research, you must first ask for his credentials; once this is established, you can look into his background. Go on the Internet and ask questions in forums: JIU-JITSU.NET provides a great service for this kind of thing. The Jiu-jitsu community is small enough so that an instructor's lineage may be easily traced by word of mouth. It is important to familiarize yourself with any subject before making a large financial and life altering commitment. If after doing your research, you are still unsure about your potential instructor's credentials, ask for his instructor's information. Remember that you are interviewing him as a customer and it is not the other way around. There is a huge problem in North America right now with people who have a background in some other martial art, then

turn around and start teaching "Grappling" or Jiu-jitsu because they want your money. It is much better to learn Jiu-jitsu from a legit blue or purple belt in Brazilian Jiu-jitsu than someone who wears a black belt in something else and claims to teach Jiu-jitsu but has little or no formal training. Someone who has never spent time on the mats in regular classes as a white belt, then a blue belt (passing through the ranks) cannot possibly understand the needs of a student in this art. Your best bet is to find a school with a legitimate Brazilian Jiu-jitsu Black Belt present or a school where a Black Belt shows up to teach at least once a month and leaves a purple or brown belt to do the daily instruction. Ignore the trophies. Trophies are the most deceptive things in martial arts today. If you go to any tournament in the United States (I say United States, because it isn't always like this in Brazil), almost every child gets a 'don't cry' trophy that the instructor will keep at the school to make him look better. Of course, trophies and medals are earned and their presence at a school may be an indicator of a teacher's ability to produce champions.

But because of the "bad apples" that ruin it for the rest of us, these awards cannot be a strong deciding factor while choosing a school. Through hard work and dedication, most champions are made by themselves. No one can force someone to come to class. Great champions and great teachers are two different things; once in a blue moon, they are one and the same, but as often as a fight goes to the ground, they are not. Look for a great teacher; ignore his fight record because it has nothing to do with it. I have attended a few schools that aren't good because the teacher whose name is in the window is never there.

Don't follow the name, follow the person; you want a teacher who will get behind your name, be there for you on a daily basis to monitor your progress and help show you all that you can be.

Make sure the school has good mats and good people. No egos or bad attitudes, the students are a reflection of the teacher. If you feel like the students are going too hard on you, they probably are and you shouldn't go back. Everyone who trains with you should, at some point, beat you. After doing so they should show you how they did it so that you can learn and progress, that is the point.

How much should I pay?

Good Jiu-jitsu isn't cheap, and it shouldn't be. You will probably pay between $100 and $150 per month for two to three days per week at a good school on the east and west coasts of the United States. As you get into the middle of the country, Jiu-jitsu is cheaper, but so is everything else. If you think $100 is a lot, think about how much you spend on beer, movies or video games.

Most schools will offer different programs and price plans for training. The general rule of thumb is, the more you commit the better deal you get, for example, a regular one time class fee at an established BJJ academy is usually around $25, but the average price per month for a couple of days per week of training is around $100.

Should I Sign a Contract?

Some schools may require you to sign contracts; this is a standard practice in the martial arts business that some Brazilian Jiu-jitsu schools are beginning to adopt. There are a variety of opinions on this matter, but really the truth of the matter is this: most people when given the responsibility to pay on time, will not hold up to their end of the bargain. This is a fact and something every professional school has to be ready to deal with. As a school owner, you should know this, as a consumer you should make your decision to join a outside the pressure of a salesperson and make your decision only after shopping around. Common contracts run for six to twelve month terms and usually allow you to pay monthly via checking account (electronic funds transfer) or credit card. This practice is overall beneficial to the school and the student, ensuring a steady flow of income that any school needs to survive and grow. The 'shady' reputation of contracts typically comes from some American 'Karate' (using Karate as a generic term as many commercial schools do) schools that use the contract as a way to sell the black belt to a prospective customer.

There is a tape series made by Y.K Kim, a Tae Kwon Do businessman called "Success in the Martial Arts Business" that every martial artist should watch. The video will help both the martial arts school owner and consumer understand the business and how it works while revealing some eye opening business practices that, depending on your ethical standards, will entice or alarm you. My advice to a consumer is to take the following things as a sign to proceed with caution: 1.High-pressure sales. 2. Guarantee of a black belt within a

specific amount of time. **3.** Condescending sales people. **4.** Unclear associations or lack of credentials. Every school needs to be commercial to the point where it does not become more important than the education of the students.

Basic Dojo Etiquette

These are some general rules to follow during training:

- Keep your uniform clean.
- Avoid foul language.
- Respect everyone.
- Never challenge an instructor to a fight. (Ask politely for help.)
- Be on time for class.
- Call your instructor if you will be absent for a length of time.
- Always bow or shake hands before sparring.
- NEVER get too aggressive while sparring, you should relax and go easy - don't grind away, or go too hard trying to tap people out.
- No Shoes on the mat.
- Refrain from horseplay, talking, and interrupting while your instructor is teaching.
- Keep yourself properly groomed.

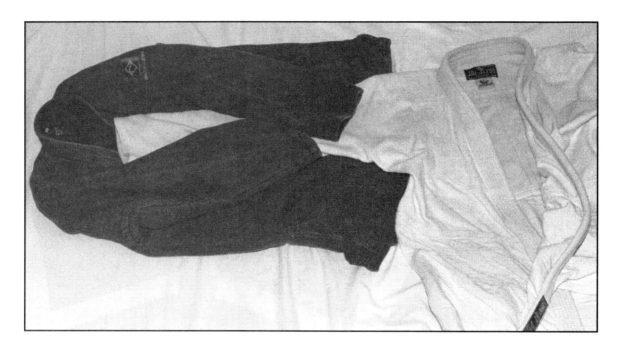

Your Kimono

The official uniform of Jiu-jitsu in which you will be training is called a "Kimono" or "Gi". This uniform consists or 3 pieces: a jacket or top, a pair of drawstring pants (usually padded at the knees) and a belt. The uniform is made out a specially weaved cotton material that will be able to withstand the rigorous practice of Jiu-jitsu without immediately tearing. Your Kimono should be kept as clean as possible and treated as your armor. As you practice Jiu-jitsu, you will find it useful as both an offensive and defensive tool. You will also realize its value as a common uniform to promote safe and technical practice of Jiu-jitsu.

For now, you should view your kimono as a set of training wheels. As you develop a higher level of proficiency, you will learn to perform Jiu-jitsu techniques both with and without a kimono. For now, the kimono will add a level of sophistication to your game that will result in you as a student becoming a more advanced and technical fighter. After you progress to blue belt level, you will be ready for The Master Text; where you will be introduced to a large number of techniques that do not require the use of the kimono.

Basic Concept of Belts

The ranking system in Brazilian Jiu-jitsu is done through a series of colored belts. Each belt represents a level of proficiency. Each belt generally takes between 2 and 5 years of consistent practice to obtain.

This is from the Gracie website:

"It typically takes between six and fifteen years to achieve a black belt from the Federacao. All promotions involving any black belt rank require the recommendation of two masters and the approval of at least five officials of the Federacao. Ranks below black belt are awarded by individual professors and are then confirmed publicly through competition with other students of the same rank. Beginners and new students wear a white belt. Adult belt levels progress from a white belt to a blue belt, and then a purple belt, and finally brown belt, after which the practitioner becomes eligible for a black belt. There are a larger number of belt colors for children."

College analogy:

One way to help beginners understand how the belts work in Brazilian Jiu-jitsu is to compare them to college degrees. They are similar in length of time and meaning. A blue belt can be compared to an associate's degree. It usually takes around two years to achieve this level and the level of proficiency the degree represents is similar. A purple belt can be compared to a bachelor's degree: this is a degree that takes four years to achieve and represents an almost identical level of proficiency, especially in the field of teaching; where this level allows you to become a teacher so long as you continue your education. A brown belt can be compared to a master's degree, especially in length of time (around six to eight years, two to four years after a bachelor's degree is obtained). A black belt in Brazilian Jiu-jitsu is similar to a PHD in most respects: this level allows you to teach independently and represents a true mastery of the art. The length of time behind a belt is very important, you must spend a sufficient amount of time at each level to ensure maturity both mentally and physically.

17

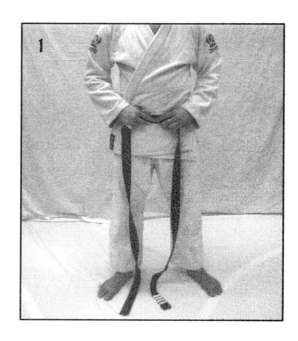

Tying the Belt

Unlike your Kimono, your belt should never be washed. Its natural soiling and wear is a symbol of your hard work, dedication to practice and time spent in the dojo (school).

The text below is a description of pictures 1 & 2 on the left and 3 - 10 on the next two pages.

Close the front of your kimono, left side over the right. Find the center of your belt and place it at the center of your stomach as shown in **figure 1**.

Wrap the belt completely around your back until both ends are in front of you again. One side should be under the other.

Now thread the right side of the belt end over the left.

To complete the square knot, loop the left end of the belt over the right to complete the knot.

Warm Ups and Stretching

A steak pulled straight from the freezer is less pliable than it is after it is defrosted. Muscle tissue is much like a piece of meat; while cold, it is not flexible and may actually become brittle. Once the muscle tissue is warmed, its range of motion will become much greater, facilitating an increase in physical activity required for Jiu-jitsu practice.

Before you stretch, you must warm your muscles slowly. The "defrosting" cycle or warm up that precedes stretching should last anywhere from five to fifteen minutes, depending on the individual and intensity of both the following activity and the current warm up. The warm-up should consist of any low impact aerobic activity, such as jogging or jumping jacks.

Once you are properly warmed up, you may begin to slowly stretch your muscles and tendons in order to prepare them for the strains of Jiu-jitsu practice. Stretching should be performed slowly and cautiously with great attention paid to any abnormality or discomfort.

Commonly overlooked by many athletes is the importance of stretching after a training session. Stretching afterwards will aid in the recovery time of muscles, increase in range of motion and future flexibility and overall strength.

Once you are ready for The Master Text, you will learn about methods of physical training with and without special equipment that will maximize your performance during Jiu-jitsu practice.

The Art of "Falling"

"Ukemi" is the Japanese term to describe the art of "falling". Becoming proficient at these techniques will allow you to practice safely with greater frequency.

This first example is an illustration of how to fall backward properly without sustaining injury.

The following text describes pictures one and two on my left: First, I stand in a natural posture with my feet about shoulder width apart and my knees slightly bent.

Squat until your thigh is just about horizontal with the floor. Your hands should be in front of you for balance, palms down. During exercise, I might not want my knees to extend over the front of my toes, but because I am only supporting my body weight, excess pressure on my knees in minimal. Keep your posture straight by looking straight ahead and curving your lower back in (chest out, head up).

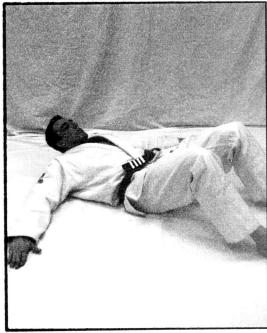

At this point, let yourself roll backward to the floor. You will now curve your back, keeping your head off the floor (chin to your chest). Do not fall on the floor with your back flat.

Keep your hands in front of you as you fall. Do not let your knees come up at your face. Picture 3 is a short period of time between the squatting position and picture 4.

In order to land safely, you will "break your fall" by slapping your hands on the floor at either side of your body. Your palms should be facing down and your arms should be stretched out at about a 45 degree angle. For this fall (the rear fall), the angle of your arms will usually slap the mat naturally at an angle slightly greater than 45 degrees in order to properly stop the momentum of your body falling back to the mat.

Keep your head up and let your air out as you fall. Although you let your air out, keep your teeth closed to avoid biting your tongue.

Falling to the Side

The next four frames illustrate the proper method of falling to the side safely.

Once again, stand in a natural, relaxed posture with your back straight and your knees slightly bent. Your feet should be about shoulder width apart and your hands at your sides.

To let yourself fall to the mat, you will bend your left knee slightly. At the same time, you will bring your right arm up with your palm facing the floor.

Your right leg should now begin to move to the left, intentionally removing the base on your right side. As your right foot advances upward and to the side you will lower your body slightly by bending at the knee.

The motion created by your right hand and left should be done simultaneously.

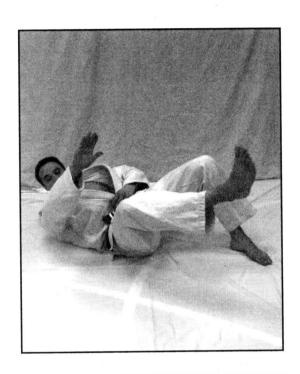

Once you fall to the floor, you will execute the same type of technique used to fall back. You should keep your head from hitting the floor, your teeth closed and you should let your air out as you fall.

In order to break your fall, you will slap the mat with your right hand, palm down at a 45 degree angle.

Note:

Do not cross your left leg over your right leg as shown below.

Rolling Forward

In order to begin this technique, you will prepare your body by stepping forward slightly out of your natural posture with your left leg. You will tuck your chin to your chest as you did previously.

Your left elbow should point out in front of you as the hand of the same arm faces the floor, palm down. You should now be making a circle with your arms as shown in figure 1.

Bend your the knee of your left leg and begin to lean forward until your left palm reaches the floor. Your right palm should be facing the the floor and the wall behind you - this is the hand you will slap the mat with once you complete the roll.

Try to make a circle with your body so that you do not smash your elbow or knee on the floor in front of you.

As you roll forward, do so over your shoulder, not your head.

You will now reach toward your right foot with your left hand to properly roll over.

As you roll over your back, it should be curved, not flat. During the landing, you should let the air escape from your lungs and slap the mat as shown at a 45 degree angle. Slapping the mat in this way will save you from the possibility of landing on a braced arm, which could cause serious injury to your elbow, shoulder and wrist. Your head should not touch the floor through this entire process.

Once you become comfortable with these Ukemi techniques, you will be able to practice takedowns and throws free from the fear of falling that normally accompanies untrained practice. This liberation of fear will clear your mind and allow you to concentrate on better technique.

Brazilian Jiu-jitsu Basics

Standing Techniques Chapter Outline

Closing Distance   Punch Defense   Kick Defense

Grab Defenses   Rear Choke Defense

BearHug
Defense

Head Lock
Defense

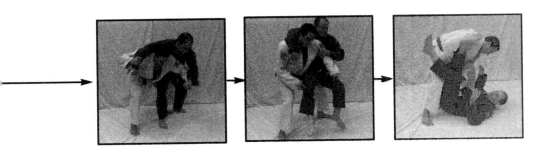

Techniques from the Standing Position:

As a beginner, much of your practice will be isolated to one specific area of concentration for a particular class period. Since the focus of Brazilian Jiu-jitsu for beginners is on groundwork and the body positioning that occurs there, much of your "sparring" or free practice with resistance will occur with both participants starting on the knees. There are many reasons for this that you will come to understand over time, but to provide you with a simple understanding: the more comfortable you are on the ground, the more relaxed you will be about engaging in the practice of Jiu-jitsu with full resistance. Many participants are also initially hesitant due to a natural feeling of cluster phobia that occurs while someone is pinning you on the floor. This hesitation is relieved by the separation of specific positions during training and practice. Another reason for this separation is to "force" students to move away from areas of natural skill in order to develop their weaker areas. This complete development of Jiu-jitsu's basic techniques is important before moving on to more advanced techniques. Some students who may not be very proficient on the ground may choose to stay standing if given the opportunity while "sparring" starts standing. This may occur due to a natural fear of "losing" or elevated ego. Therefore, instructors of Brazilian Jiu-jitsu will usually start free sparring sessions on the knees and standing at separate times.

In this next section, I have isolated the basic standing techniques of Jiu-jitsu that most beginners will encounter during their first year of training. Practical application and basic understanding of these techniques is required by most instructors before promotion to blue belt can occur.

Quedas

Called "quedas' in Brazilian Portuguese, takedowns or throws are standing methods of attack and defense whose purpose is to bring an attacker to the ground through the use of balance, timing and leverage. In most cases, Jiu-jitsu practitioners utilize basic principles of physics such as momentum, gravity and acceleration to achieve the throw with minimum effort and maximum efficiency.

greatly reduced. After a level of safety is achieved by the use of this position, a skilled Jiu-jitsu fighter will take his opponent to the floor where any of the "ground positions" previously soon to be detailed will be used.

Getting to the Clinch

Many great champions of Jiu-jitsu through its recent history have said, "If you have the clinch, you have good Jiu-jitsu." This is a theme that resounds strongly through the art's value as a tool for self-defense. The principle theory is this: In any style of fighting, whether the intention of the combatants is to achieve victory through the implementation of strikes or submission holds, one thing is inevitable: most of the time, the participants will clinch. Clinching is simply when both partners "hold" each other while standing. Once a Jiu-jitsu practitioner achieves the clinch, the ability of his opponent to strike with a great deal of force (damaging force) is

Getting to the Clinch

In this example to the left, I am using a method of progressive indirect attack to create an opening so that I may safely achieve the clinch position.

In **figure 1**, I throw a high strike to my opponent's head. It is not my intention to strike my opponent. My intention is to give my opponent time to raise his hand to defend my strike. By raising his hand, he will create an opening at his waist where his arm would normally be blocking me from "entering". You will notice that I control his right hand with my left hand as I throw the strike so that my opponent does not strike me with that hand as I close the distance.

In **figure 2**, I control his arm as I finish closing the distance, placing my head on his chest. My left hand will wrap around my opponent's waits so he cannot move back and away from me, creating distance that will enable him to strike.

Getting to the Clinch 2 (Baiting)

This method of getting to the clinch is a "baiting method". In this situation, I place my legs at a close distance to my opponent, but lean back slightly so that my head is just out of my opponent's reach. In order to encourage my opponent to attempt a strike to my head, I lower my hands away from my face. Two things make it safe for me to do so:

-My head is out of his reach.

-I am anticipating the strike to my head.

Once my opponent throws the strike (**figure 2**), I lean forward. As I lean forward, I keep my hands up to protect my face from both kicks and punches.

As I "enter" in **figure 3**, I hold him with my left hand to prevent him from moving back and control his arm with my right arm. I place my head to his chest in order to protect my face from punches.

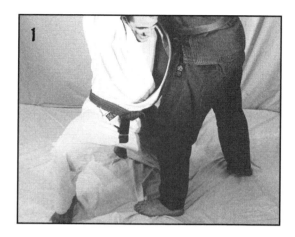

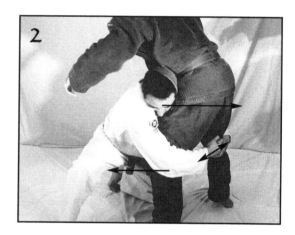

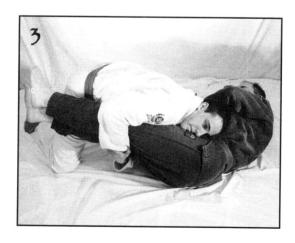

Takedowns from the Clinch

Once I have reached the clinch position, I must use it to my advantage. illustrated in **figure 1**, I drop to one knee. I do so with my chest very close to my opponent's leg, leaving him with very little space to strike.

Next (**figure 2**), I hug my opponent's legs at the knees, clasping both hands.

Once I have control of his legs, I squeeze my arms together, narrowing my opponent's base. Once my opponent's base is weak, I will drive my head forward, pushing off my right leg for power and simultaneously pull his legs toward me.

This movement will cause my opponent to fall backward (**figure 3**). As my opponent falls, I will hug his legs tightly, squeezing them together as I move around to one side of his body in order to control him.

Defending a Punch (O Goshi)

In this situation, my opponent attempts to punch me at a closer range. To defend, I raise my left hand to my left ear, protecting the entire left side of my head (**figure 1**). To protect myself from potential counter strikes on my right side, I grab my opponent's left hand.

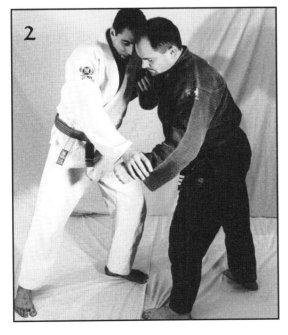

Illustrated in **figure 2**, I push my opponent's left hand down slightly to create space for me to "enter". I will also wrap my left arm over and around my opponent's right arm.

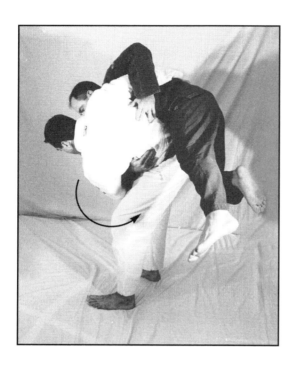

In order to lift my opponent off the ground, I turn, facing the same direction as him. During this turn, I keep my hips lower than his and "bump" into him, off-balancing my opponent. My right arm goes under his left arm and to his back while my left arm pulls his right to my waist.

To flip him over my back (hips) and throw him to the floor, I pull down and to the left with my left arm. At the same time, I twist my hips to the right (counter clock-wise).

Once my opponent has landed in front of me, I must assume a position of control. In this case, I have chosen knee on belly, which will be discussed in greater detail later on in this text.

Basic Kick Defense

In this situation, I have not yet had the opportunity to create an opening to clinch. Before I can set anything up, my opponent throws a kick.

There are a few very important factors that must be present in my initial defense: First, both of my hands must remain up at either side of my face to protect it from strikes (**figure 1**). Second, I will use my legs, not my hands to defend myself from this kick, since it is low (**figure 2**).

The reasons for this method of defense become clear when you consider that by "dropping" my hands away from my face to defend the kick initially, my opponent might chamber his kick and land a second one to my head. My opponent might also be setting me up with a combination of kicks and punches, hoping that by kicking low, I will reach for his leg. If I reach for his leg, I will create an opportunity for my opponent to land a punch to my undefended face.

As I lift my left leg to defend, I make sure my knee is raised above my waistline and my toes are pointed down. My right (rear) leg is bent slightly at the knee for extra balance and shock absorbancy. You will notice that in **figure 3**, I keep my right hand up to defend my face. My left hand now reaches down to grab my opponent's right ankle.

Once I secure my opponent's ankle, I will step forward, hooking my right leg behind my opponent's left. I step forward enough so that my belly is touching my opponent's inner right leg. (**figure 4**).

To bring my opponent to the floor, I will use a technique that comes from Judo called *O Uchi Gari*. In order to perform this movement, I Push my opponent's chest forward with my right arm (I may also push his face for extra effect if desired), I pull my opponent's right leg with my left arm and simultaneously hook my right leg behind his left knee and kick back (**figure 5**). A counter clock-wise twisting motion may be employed in order to provide me with extra momentum during the application of this technique.

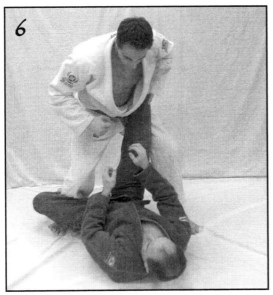

Once my opponent lands (**figure 6**), I may pass his guard, ankle lock him or strike my opponent from the top. These methods of follow-up attack will be discussed later in this text.

Basic Throat or Lapel Grab Defense

In this next segment, I will illustrate a defense against a common lapel or throat grab. This is a very unique defense that I have not seen elsewhere. I learned this technique while studying a classical form of Jiu-jitsu and believe it to be very effective in the event that a person attacks you in this way.

One important thing to remember is that at any time, you may simply strike your opponent to the face in order to release this hold. If his arms are grabbing you, they are not defending a strike to the face. If you strike your opponent to the face, he will have to release his hold to defend himself or be hit.

Some practitioners of Jiu-jitsu are against methods of striking. It is an issue that I have gone into great detail about philosophically in The Master Text, but the purpose of this book is simply to illustrate basic techniques.

To begin this movement, I control my opponent's right hand with my left (**figure 3**). Note that I will not let go of this hand throughout the course of the entire technique - this is important. My right arm reaches over my opponent's left arm until my right hand is pointing down between my opponent's arms.

In **figure 4**, I step forward slightly with my right leg and thrust my right hand between my opponent's arms, passing my right side to my opponent's left. I duck my head under his right armpit while still controlling his right arm. This control of the right arm will be important later to finish him, but is crucial now to protect myself from potential chokes that my opponent may choose to apply.

By practicing this technique, you will notice that if it is being performed on you, your right wrist will begin to twist if you choose to continue holding my jacket. Once you master this movement, you may try it quickly in oder to actually flip your opponent over.

I will continue to step through in a counter clock-wise motion until I am positioned as shown in **figure 5**. You will notice that because I performed this movement slowly, my opponent had the opportunity to let go of my lapel with his left hand.

I will not give him the same option with his right hand. I secure my opponent's right hand as shown here and begin to push his elbow down and forward. Take note of this grip I am using on my opponent's right hand - I have switched from the sleeve to the knife edge of his hand. My palm is over the top of his hand with my fingers gripping the pinky-side of his hand. This will allow me to twist his wrist, bending his arm in such a way that his elbow will point up. The pain at his wrist will cause most to submit at this point.

In **figure 6**, I step behind him, creating pressure on his wrist as I just described and his shoulder by pushing his elbow down and pulling up on his hand.

Rear Choke Defense

In this situation, my opponent has secured an arm around my neck from behind. This is a typical "street hold" that all Jiu-jitsu students must learn to defend against.

In **figure 1**, I begin to set up my defense by bending my knees and positioning my hips to the right. I grab his sleeve at the shoulder with my right hand and pull down. I also grab his wrist with my left hand as shown.

In **figure 2**, I drop my hips below his by bending my knees and squatting down. To avoid additional pressure on my neck during this movement, I will continue to pull down on my opponent's right arm with both of my arms.

After I lower my hips below my opponent's belt line, I will make a move to lift my opponent onto my hips. Shown to the left in **figure 3**, I do so by straightening my legs and leaning forward slightly. I am still pulling down on my opponent's arms to assist the lift and take pressure off the choke.

I will now "throw" my opponent over my back with the "seoi nage" movement (**figure 4**). To do so, I will pull my opponent's arm down and to my right, leading him to my right side. I will also make a slight twisting motion to the right with my hips to roll him over my shoulder and back.

As I complete the throw, my opponent will land directly in front of me, being flipped over my front. I continue to secure his arm for potential follow-up techniques in case the throw has not neutralized his desire to fight (**figure 5**).

Rear Choke Defense 2

In this situation, my opponent pushes the back of my leg with his foot. Because he is doing this, I can not lean forward to flip him over my head (**figure 1**).

To begin my defense, I pull down on his right arm as I did during the first choke defense.

Since I cannot pull my opponent over my head, I pull my opponent's right elbow into my chest and begin to turn to my right. As I turn, I lean forward and secure his right wrist with my left hand (**figure 2**). I try to keep his right arm at an angle to create pressure on his shoulder.

Some less experienced opponent's will submit or fall to the floor because of the pressure created on the right shoulder when this move is properly applied. The proper application of this movement will come in time with a great deal of sensitivity and practice.

The pressure created on my opponent's right shoulder will cause him to lose his balance to the right side of his body.

I will take advantage of this loss of balance by hooking my right leg behind his right leg (**figure 4**). When I do so, I must be sure to pass my centerline beyond his and lean forward so he cannot counter my throw.

At this point, I will use the O Soto Gari technique by kicking my right leg up and back, reaping my opponent's right leg. As I do this, I drive my right shoulder into his right shoulder and maintain pressure on his shoulder.

The combination of the movements described above will cause my opponent to fall to the floor as shown in **figure 5**. Once my opponent is on the floor, I will secure his arm for potential follow-up techniques.

Bear Hug from Behind

In this situation, My opponent is holding my from behind. He has both of my arms trapped by wrapping his arms around my entire body.

My first priority is to "break his grip" so that I may begin to escape. To do so, I will first take a very deep breath in, filling my lungs completely with air and expanding my diaphragm as much as possible. This will cause my opponent to widen his grip.

Once my chest is expanded, I will make my move to escape. All in one move, I will combine the following steps: I let out my air, becoming instantly smaller than I was before. I Squat to the floor, lowering my base, as shown in **Figure 2**. I spread my arms apart as shown here to the left. I will also drive my butt into his hips ar I drop my weight. The combination of these above moves done simultaneously with proper speed and force will break my opponent's hold.

After I break my opponent's grip, I control both of his hands as shown here in **figure 3**. It is very important to control the wrists or hands of my opponent to ensure that he does not use them in order to choke me or start a new attack.

Once I have control of his hands, I will then step to the side, leading with my hips out (**figure 3**).

Once I have made the appropriate amount of room with my hips to facilitate this next move, I will step behind him with my left leg (**figure 4**). At this point it is crucial that I control my opponent's right arm so that he does not grab my head. In the event that he does, the next technique will come in handy.

I will now squat slightly, bumping my left leg into the back of his body, off-balancing him. I will make a sort of "chair" for him to make it easy to support his weight.

At this point, I no longer need to concern myself with his arms. I will now grab both of his legs as shown here to the left and begin to pull him up, back and to my left.

The finish is obvious and simple. I will lift and turn him until I have enough height and leverage to "dump" him on his head or back.

Head Lock Escape

In this situation, my opponent has secured a head-lock however, the fact he is standing in front of me will make is easy for me to escape.

The first thing I do is secure a grip on his right wrist with my right hand. Doing this will ensure that he cannot create additional pressure on my face or skull and will also stop him from sliding his arm down to my neck and choking me.

The next step in my move to escape is as I continue to pull on his wrist with my right hand, I place my left arm as far as I can over his shoulder. Once my left arm is extended over my opponent's right shoulder, I will begin to push forward, down and out ant an angle with the ridge of my hand (pinky side) against the side of his face.

At this point, I will begin to posture up. This action of looking up will help to completely release the grip my opponent has on my neck.

As I look up (**figure 3**), I begin to turn my left wrist so that my palm faces downward. The twisting motion is important technically because it will actually increase my power to move my opponent's head.

I use the twisting-move to spin my opponent around as shown here in **figure 4**.

Once my opponent is facing me, I secure the thumb-side of my forearm under his chin so that it is touching the front of my opponent's throat. I squeeze my arm tightly around his neck and keep his head trapped under my armpit.

Once my arm is secured tightly around my opponent's neck, I place my right hand on his shoulder as shown.

I will then place my left palm on my right wrist as shown in **figure 6** and in the highlighted circle.

To tighten the choke, creating additional pressure on my opponent's neck, I will do the following:

Make a reverse "motor-cycle-rev" move with my left hand around my right. This will lift my left wrist a few inches, tightening the choke around my opponent's neck. Next I will squeeze my arm around his neck tighter and arch my body up and back.

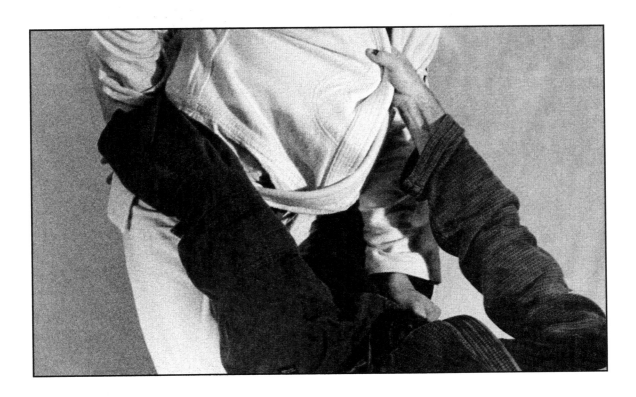

Passing The Guard

Because the guard is a great place from which to launch an effective attack, it would be safe to assume that you won't want to be inside it (between your opponent's legs). The following are some methods of "passing the guard" or escaping from between your opponent's legs.

Passing the guard is usually achieved in a basic four-step process: First, you must maintain a good defensive posture to make it difficult for your opponent to achieve an arm lock, choke you or turn you over. Second, you must uncross your opponent's ankles if they are locked behind your back. Third, you must control your opponent's hips; the hips are the center of your opponent's body and will determine the level of usage he will have with his legs to control you. The fourth step is most commonly referred to as "passing the legs", this is the process of moving your body from between your opponent's legs to a top position at his side.

Passing the Guard Chapter Outline

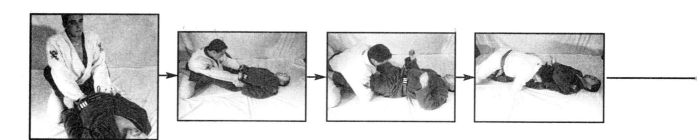

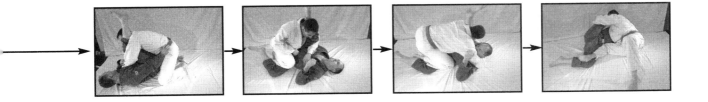

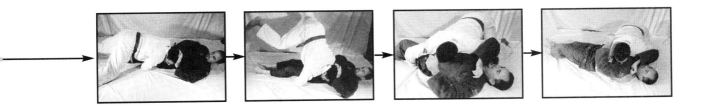

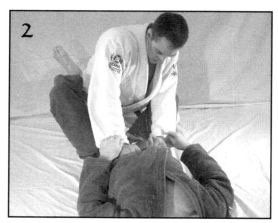

Guard Pass from the Knees

Often called the "classic Pass', this is a very basic but effective guard pass from the knees.

First, I establish a wide base with my knees (**figure 1**), sitting back on my feet to ensure that my opponent does not sweep me (turn me over) from his guard.

Once my base is established, I will begin to push on his abdominal region with my palms as in **figure 2**. I may hold his belt or pants to prevent my opponent from pulling my arms toward his head and disturbing my base. I will continue to push down on his belly and move my legs to a 45 degree angle, making an "L" with my right knee in his butt. My left leg will angle out for balance and support. As I create this wedge between my opponent and I, pressure must be constant on my opponent's belly. By pressing down and moving my body away from his, my opponent will be forced to uncross his ankles.

Once the ankles are uncrossed, I will place one arm under his leg as shown in **figure 3**.

As I place my arm under my opponent's leg, it is very important not to allow him to control my right arm and pull it inside his guard (**figure 4**).

To prevent the triangle choke, I hold his belt or pants and continue pressing on my opponent's abdomen with my right hand. I then move my opponent's left leg onto my left shoulder while controlling his hips with both hands as shown in **figure 5**. To disable my opponent's maneuverability, I pull his hips toward me. It is crucial that I look up at this point and keep my butt to the floor.

My posture at this point is essential. As long as I maintain good posture, it will be impossible for my opponent to secure a triangle choke or armlock.

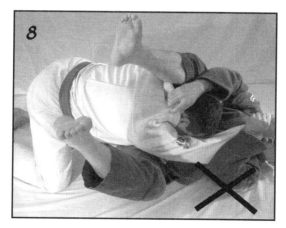

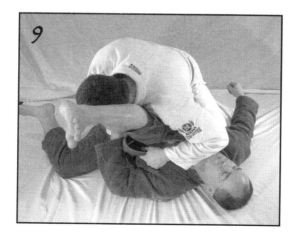

In these next two pictures to the left (**figures 7 and 8**), I am illustrating the result of poor posture. You will notice how I have allowed my butt to move away from my heels and I am leaning forward. This is very wrong during this pass. As you can see, improper posture will allow my opponent to secure a triangle choke or pull my right arm inside his legs and secure an armlock.

In the last frame (**figure 9**) on this page, I am continuing to pass my opponent's guard. I will do so by creating pressure on the back of his left leg. I "smash" it toward his face as I drive my left forearm into his neck. My right arm will continue to control his hips to prevent a counter. I will now move my butt from my heels to create pressure, but not before I am ready to perform this part of the movement correctly.

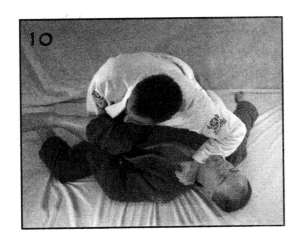

In order to "Pass" my opponent's leg, I look up and turn my face away (**figure 10**). I continue to create pressure using my left forearm on my opponent's neck.

Once my opponent's right leg is "passed", I will shift my body toward my opponent's head in order to secure a better hold (**figure 11**).

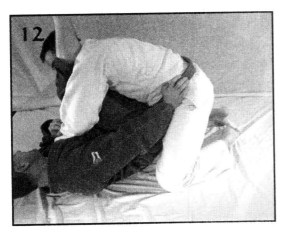

Sometimes as you are trying to pass your opponent's right leg, he will stop you by placing his right hand in your hip as shown in **figure 12** and extending his own hips. The next page will cover the appropriate resolution to this typical counter …

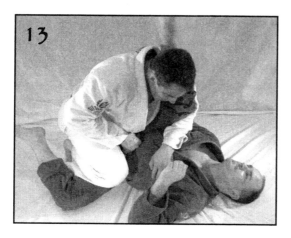

Instead of forcing my way around my opponent, I will now place my right shin over my opponent's left leg. It is important that I keep my right foot hooked on one side of my opponent's leg and my knee touching the floor on the other (**figure 13**). This will trap his leg and prevent other possible counters.

At this point, I will reach forward and clasp both hands behind my opponent's neck, smashing his knee to his face. Notice in **figure 14** how my right leg is still controlling my opponent's left leg as described above.

To bring my body around my opponent and establish a position of control at his side, I switch my base by bringing one leg over the other. I do this by maintaining control and laying on my right side. As I do this, I drive my right shoulder into my opponent's face to maintain pressure and stop him from sitting up (**figure 15**).

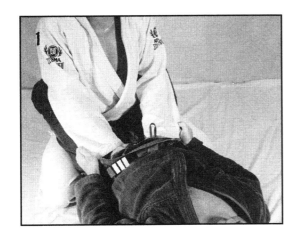

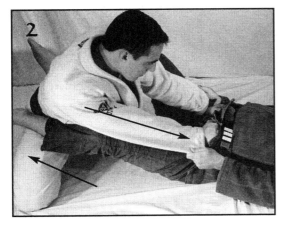

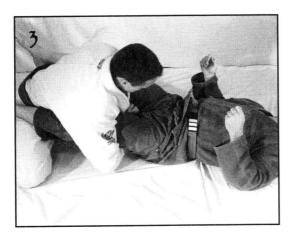

Guard Pass from the Knees 2

In this situation, I use the method of pushing down on his lower abdomen to protect my self against armlocks, chokes and sweeps. I usually grab my opponent's belt of pants in order to make it difficult for him to pull my hand off (**figure 1**).

I make an "L" with my legs with one knee in the center of my opponent's butt and the other posted out at a 45 degree angle. I then push down and at a slight angle to 'pin' my opponent's hips and move them away from me. I then slide back to break the hooks (uncross the ankles) as in **figure 2**.

Once the hooks are open, I hug his legs above the knee as shown in **figure 3**. I then grab my opponent's left leg with my right hand and his right leg with my left hand.

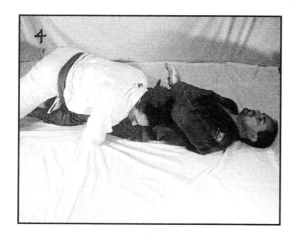

I bring my opponent's legs as close together as possible and move to a push up position. I then start to drive my head in his belly and move to his side (**figure 4**).

My opponent pushes my face to escape as shown in **figure 5**. Since I cannot proceed in that direction without resistance, I hop to the other side of his body landing in a side control position and fixing my grip on his gi.

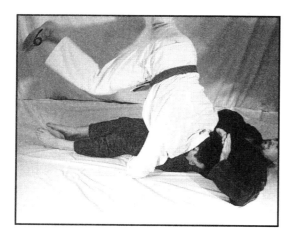

As I hop over my opponent's body, I maintains a firm grip on his legs to prevent him from regaining his guard.

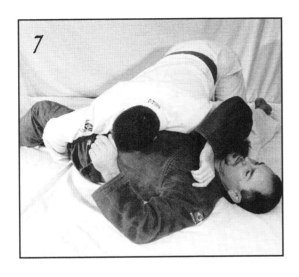

As I move around to the side of his body, note how my right arm continues to control my opponent's right leg. The reason for this is to prevent him from getting his guard back while I am trying to gain control (**figure 7**).

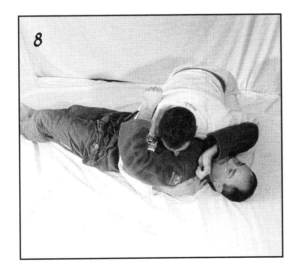

To complete this guard pass and establish control over my opponent, I move my left arm deep under my opponent's right armpit. This action will prevent him from using his hand in order to escape my hold. I will then hold him tightly with my chest to his and both hands under his armpits (**figure 8**).

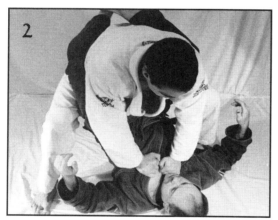

Standing Guard Pass

In this situation, I have decided to pass my opponent's guard using a "standing" method. I am holding my partner's gi with my palms down and fingers pointed in. This will ensure that he does not secure an armlock, since my elbows must be on his chest in order for him to secure an arm lock.

Once my posture is secure (**figure 2**), I hop up to my feet simultaneously. I he pulls my ankles to sweep me backward, I will pull up on his gi collars and throw my hips forward to defend the sweep and keep from falling back.

In **figure 3**, I use a combination of good posture and my back and leg muscles to lift him.

IMPORTANT!
Once I lift him up, I **MUST** press down on his hip to avoid armbars and chokes.

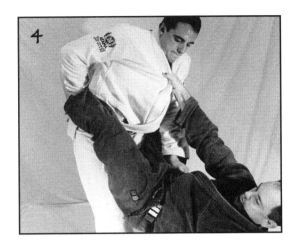

I then move my right hand behind me to break his hooks as shown here in **figure 4**. I keep pressing his hip down to avoid the triangle choke.

Once my opponent's ankles uncross, I go down with him, moving my right arm under his leg and to his collar.

I smash his leg to his face with my body weight and switch my base as shown in **figure 6** (left leg over right, then back again) until I land in side control.

Techniques from the Top Position
Controlling from the Top

Hold-downs consist of a series of immobilization techniques and body positions that will allow you to either restrain or submit your opponent from the top. Your legs should be used as both counter weights and stabilizers to hold your opponent in a desired position. Most hold-downs from the side are designed to keep your opponent's shoulders pinned to the floor.

Kesa Gatame

There are two variations of Kesa Gatame: one in which your arm is under the armpit of your opponent's far arm and the other where your arm is around his neck instead. In the variation where your arm is not under your opponent's armpit, you must be sure to keep the shoulder closest to you off the floor and maintain an upward pull on that arm. This leverage will stop your opponent from rolling on his side and escaping.

100 Kilos

This is simply a hold down from the side position where you are chest to chest with your opponent. The leg of your opponent that is closest to you should be controlled so that he cannot replace his leg underneath your body and regain his guard position. For this purpose, your hand will usually grab your opponent's pants by the hip or leg.

Sometimes when your hand is required for a finishing technique from this position, the hand is removed from the leg and the (your) leg closest to his leg is moved in to block it. The leg on the side of your opponent's head is usually kept in an extended position for two purposes:

1) To assist in creating pressure by driving off the ball of your foot.

2) To provide a counter weight in the event that your opponent attempts to roll you.

Modified Kesa Gatame

Pull up on your opponent's close arm so he cannot face you and get to his knees.

Post your leg out for a base

The difference between Kesa Gatame and Modified Kesa Gatame is the arm under your opponent's far armpit.

North South

Known in Japanese terms as "kami shiho gatame" or "top four corner hold", this position should be help by keeping a wide base with your legs. If your legs are not posted out at a 45 degree angle, your opponent will have a better chance of rolling you from side to side. Your opponent's hips will be controlled by the use of your hands and sometimes your head in his lower abdominal region. Control of the hips will restrict the lower extremities full range of motion.

Mount

If you have achieved the mount position, you will be 'sitting' on your opponent's chest with both knees on the floor at either side of his body. This position is an excellent position from which to attack because your arms are not always required to maintain the hold. The freedom of your arms will allow you to either strike your opponent or apply submission holds.

Knee on Belly

Like the mount position, your hands are free to attack your opponent with strikes or submission holds. Many experts of jiu-jitsu prefer to use this position while fighting on surfaces that may cause damage to the knees. Here, a majority of your body weight is rested on your opponent's sternum, belly or lower chest with your knee. Your other knee is kept at a 45 degree angle to your opponent's body for balance, counter-weight, and mobility.

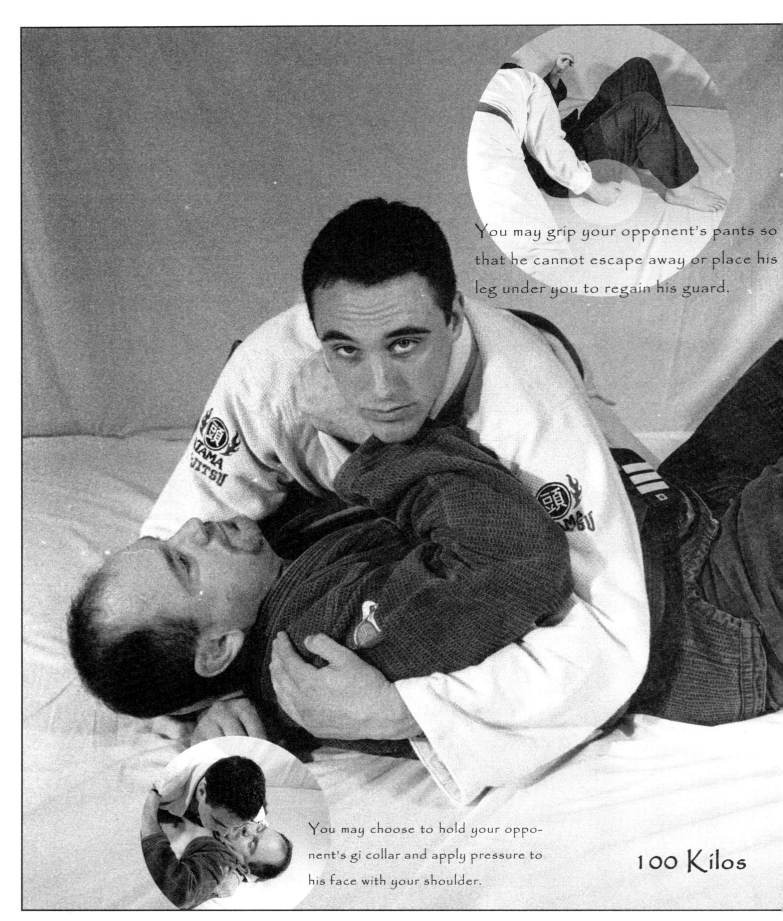

You may grip your opponent's pants so that he cannot escape away or place his leg under you to regain his guard.

You may choose to hold your opponent's gi collar and apply pressure to his face with your shoulder.

100 Kilos

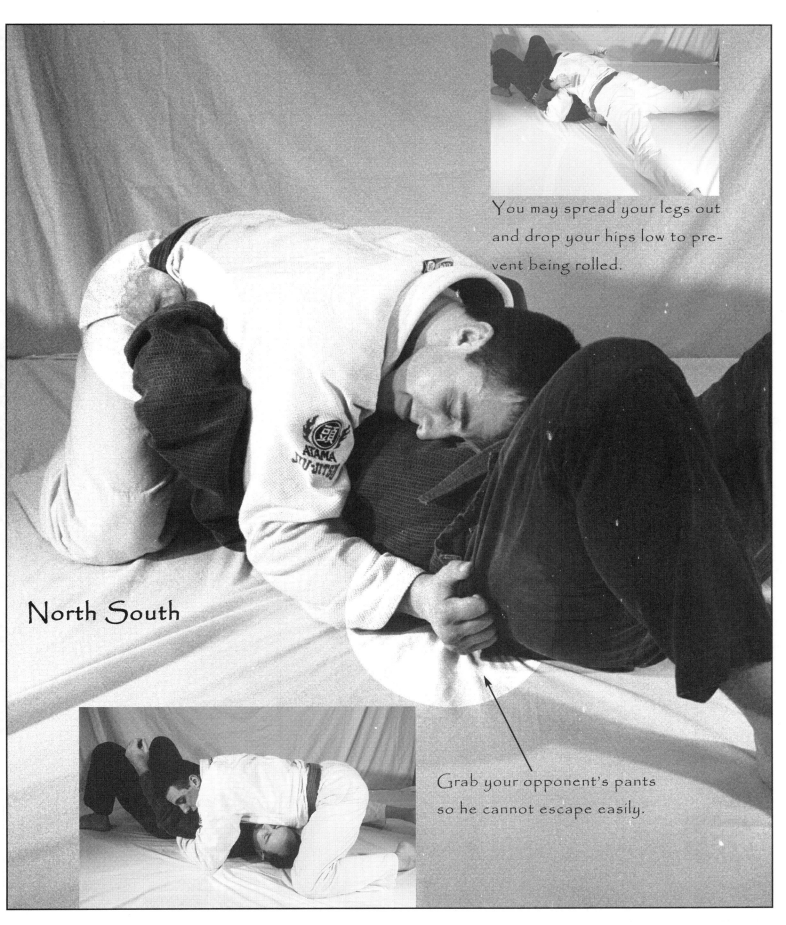

You may spread your legs out and drop your hips low to prevent being rolled.

North South

Grab your opponent's pants so he cannot escape easily.

Mount

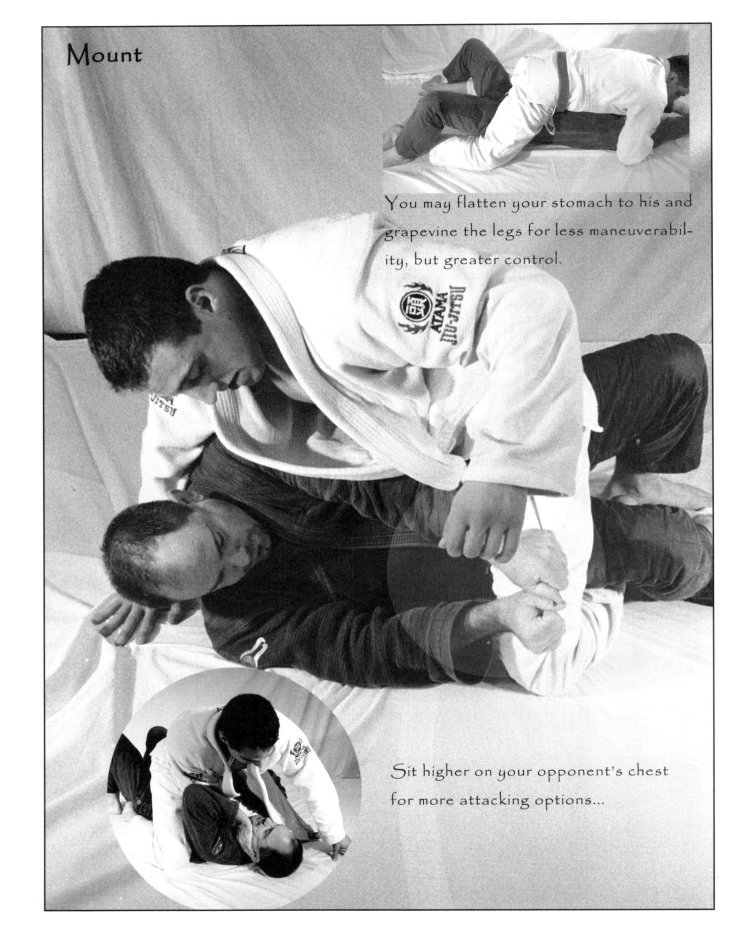

You may flatten your stomach to his and grapevine the legs for less maneuverability, but greater control.

Sit higher on your opponent's chest for more attacking options...

Your right hand may be used to control his leg or set up chokes with the use of the kimono.

Your left hand may be moved to different positions in order to establish control of set up submissions.

Hold your opponent's collar and pant leg. Pull up and drive your knee into his chest/belly for tight control.

Knee on Belly

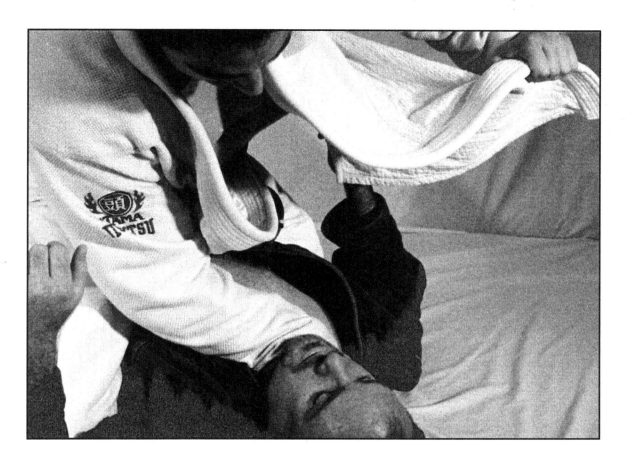

Finishing from the Top

Once you have established control of your opponent from the top position, a variety of submissions that may be applied will present themselves. The following submissions are basic joint locks and chokes which every student must know before passing on to the level of blue belt in Brazilian Jiu-jitsu.

Arm Bar
from
Mount

Americana
from
Mount

Collar
Choke
from Side

Arm Bar
from Knee
on Belly

Collar
Choke
from
Mount

Collar Choke from Knee on Belly

Kimura

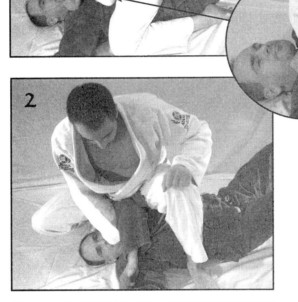

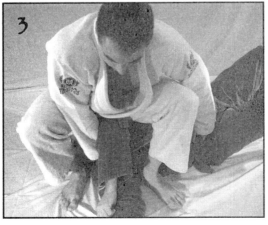

ArmBar from the Mount Position

I am mounted on my opponent's chest and he has made the mistake of "giving" me his arm by extending it toward my chest. If I choose, I may also grab his gi collar as shown in **figure 1** and press it down into his neck. This will create a choke that he will have to address. In most cases, his defense will result in the "giving" of his arm to me.

Once his arm his extended, I will pivot my body as show here in **figure 2**. I allow one of my knees to come up of the floor and the other will slide around to the top of his head. At this point I am sitting on my opponent's tricep (back of arm). Doing this will prevent my opponent from freeing his arm (getting his elbow back down to the floor).

Once the arm is secure, I will place my right foot on the right side of my opponent's face as shown in **figure 3**.

I will then hug my opponent's arm with my right arm, holding my own gi collar. I must be sure to keep his arm very near to my chest like in **figure 4**.

I will then sit down, keeping his elbow near my belly and his arm close to my chest. Both of my legs should 'pin' him down to the floor.

To finish the elbow lock, I will lay back and squeeze my knees together, keeping my opponent's thumb up. To create additional pressure, I must lift my hips and I pull his wrist toward my chest.

Americana

As a defense to the armbar, my opponent will often fold his arm so that it is not extended. I will then place both of my hands on his forearm as shown in **figure 1**, locking my elbows out so that my arms are straight.

I use the weight of my entire upper body to press his arm to the floor as shown here in **figure 2**.

Once my opponent's arm is pinned to the floor, I will bring my left elbow to the floor near my opponent's left ear (**figure 3**).

Next, I will slide my right arm under my opponent's bent left arm (**figure 4**)until I can clasp my own(left) wrist with my right hand. Once my right hand is clasping my left wrist, both elbows and knees should be firmly on the floor for balance and base as shown in **firure 5.**

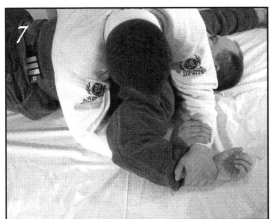

This page is dedicated to illustrating the "finishing" process of the Americana lock.

Once both elbows are on the floor I will perform the following movements to complete the lock on my opponent's left shoulder.

As shown in **figure 6**, slide his elbow toward his waist while keeping his wrist pinned. Then, lift his elbow off the floor without lifting his wrist (**figure 7**).

Some people have very flexible shoulders. If this is the case, you may create additional pressure by rotating your right hand around your left wrist like in **figure 8**. This technique will lift your opponent's left elbow off the floor an additional 2 - 3 inches creating greater pressure on his shoulder.

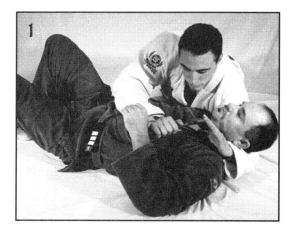

Collar Choke

In this situation, I will use my opponent's gi (kimono) to choke him. I feed my opponent's right collar with my right hand to my left hand as shown here in **figure 1**.

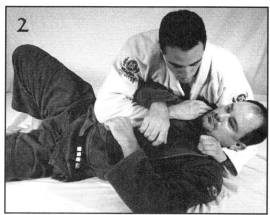

I then hook my right arm under his right arm and begin to slide my right hand behind the right side of his head. Hooking his right arm will stop him from rolling away from me and escaping as I perform the choke. My left hand is gripping my opponent's collar tightly and pulling down as shown in **figure 2**.

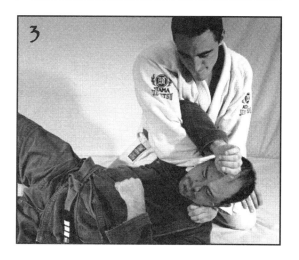

To finish the choke, I pull up on the collar with my left hand and slide down the back of his neck to my left wrist with my right hand (**figure 3**).

Collar Choke from Knee on Belly

This is a collar choke from the knee on belly position. My right hand enters his collar as shown in **figure 1**, with four fingers inside and my thumb behind his left ear.

My left hand grips his collar with my thumb inside and rotates around the left side of his neck (figure 2).

I rotate my left arm around to the front of his neck as shown in **figure 3**, and to finish, I bring my elbows down. You can sometimes slide your right knee to his left side and secure the mount for better position.

(Finish is on figure 4 of the next page)

Figure 4 (to the left) Finish of the collar choke from Knee on Belly.

Arm Lock from Knee on Belly

From **knee on belly**, my opponent (bottom) makes the mistake of putting his left hand on my knee. I hook under his left arm with my right arm as shown here in **figure 1**.

I will begin the Armlock by lifting his arm toward my chest and holding my own gi collar.

I will then begin to move around his body, stepping over his head and grab his belt or pants with my left hand as shown here in **figure 2**. Lifting my opponent's arm to my chest will make his belt easier to grab.

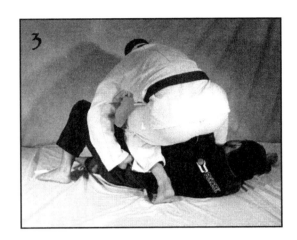

I spin around him, brining my left shin to his left side with my butt low (figure 3).

To finish, I sit down and lay back, making sure his thumb is pointed up and my knees are squeezing his arm tight as shown in **figure 4**.

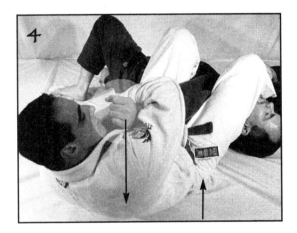

It is important to continue grabbing the belt if you do not have your left leg over his belly or he will roll out and escape.

This arm lock is called **Juji Gatame** in Japanese terminology.

Kimura

Going back to step one and two of the last movement, my opponent will turn his arm in an attempt to escape. To counter his escape and begin my next attack, I will move my left arm under his left arm as shown in **figure 1**.

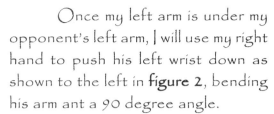

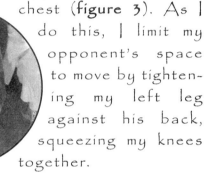

Once my left arm is under my opponent's left arm, I will use my right hand to push his left wrist down as shown to the left in **figure 2**, bending his arm ant a 90 degree angle.

Once my opponent's arm is properly bent, I will grab my right wrist with my left hand and move my opponent's arm to my chest (**figure 3**). As I do this, I limit my opponent's space to move by tightening my left leg against his back, squeezing my knees together.

To finish the Kimura Lock, I will keep his arm at a 90 degree angle and turn his wrist to my left, putting pressure on his shoulder.

Collar Choke from Mount

In this situation, I have achieved the mount position on my opponent. To start the choke, I will place my right hand deep in my opponent's collar as shown here to the left in **figure 1**.

I use my left arm to lift his chin. This makes it easier for me to place my right hand in under the left, four fingers inside. I reach as deep as I can in my opponent's collars (thumb behind the ear) and grab his collar tightly with a closed fist as in **figure 2**.

Both hands should grab the collar deep behind his ears. I make tight fists and pull my elbows toward me (**figure 3**). For balance, I drop my head to the floor.

To finish the choke, I push my chest toward his face, arch my lower back in and pull up to my back with both arms (**figure 4**).

Techniques from the Back Position

Rear Mount

Also called "taking the back", the rear mount or back mount position is a trademark position of the art of Brazilian Jiu-jitsu. This is the most dominant of all jiu-jitsu positions and will provide it's user with the most protection against counter attacks out of all the positions of jiu-jitsu. As a user of this position, you are controlling your opponent with your feet, called "hooks" over the top of his upper (front) thighs. This will limit his ability to turn freely and face you or roll away. Attacking from the back will limit your opponent's leverage to strike or attack your vital areas, while at the same time, providing you with the position in which to mount a series of highly effective attacks.

Taking the
Back from
North South

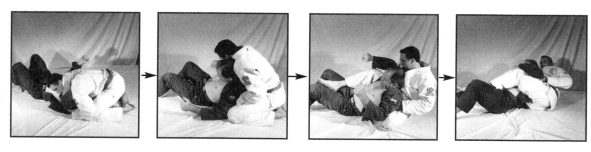

Taking
the Back

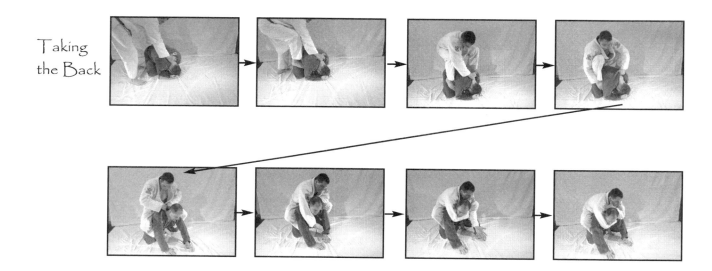

Collar
Choke from
the Back

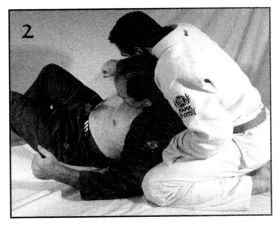

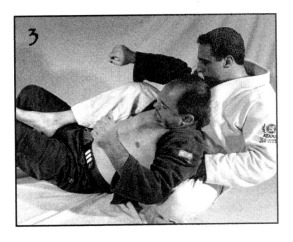

Taking the Back

From the North/South position, I will begin the taking the back section with a way to get it from top or side control.

Note for the future:
In sport, you only get the four points for taking his back if your hooks are in (your legs over the front of his) and your ankles should not be crossed. I did not want you to concentrate too much on the points system in this book, but people will usually ask why the "hooks" must be placed over the legs in this way.

Here, I am in North South position and I have both collars secured under his armpits. I lift him up on to my lap to make a little space for my next move (**figure 1**).

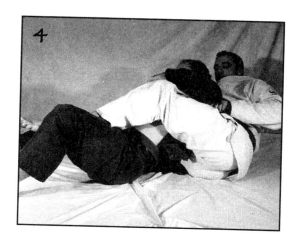

I then sit back so I can throw one hook over first, then the other while maintaining collar control as shown in **figures 2 through 4**.

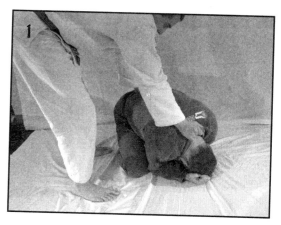

Taking the Back of a "turtled" opponent...

In this situation, my opponent has "turtled" in front of me, folding himself up into a little ball as shown in figure 1.

To begin my attack, I place my right hand in his collar and my left hand on his belt as shown in **figure 1**.

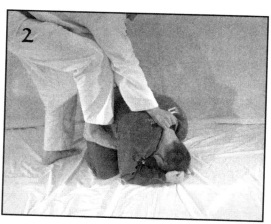

Once my hand placement is correct, I will lift his collar, creating just enough space to insert my right foot between his armpit and his right thigh (**figure 2**).

I will then move around so that I am standing on his thighs with both feet (**figure 3**).

Once I am secure, I will release my left hand from my opponent's belt and pull up on his collar like in **figure 4**.

At the same time I pull up on the collar, I will push my feet down to the floor (**figure 5**). This action will allow me to place my "hooks" over his legs and assume the "back mount" position.

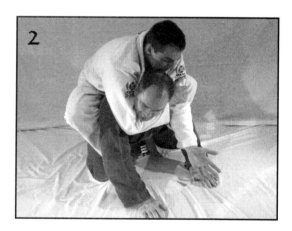

Mata Leo Choke

Once I have achieved the back mount position, I will attempt a choke to finish my opponent and end the fight.

In order to choke my opponent, I will place my right arm over his right shoulder as shown in **figure 1**. I will place my right arm under my opponent's chin with the inside of my arm touching his neck.

Once my right arm is wrapped around my opponent's neck, I will grab my left bicep with my right hand as shown in **figure 2**.

After my right arm is touching my left bicep, I will place the back of my left hand behind my opponent's head as shown in **figure 3**.

This page is devoted to the details required to finish the Mata Leo choke from the back position.

Now I put my left hand behind my opponent's head, with the palm facing me as shown in **figure 4**. I will now make a fist.

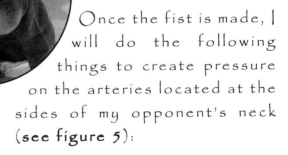

Once the fist is made, I will do the following things to create pressure on the arteries located at the sides of my opponent's neck (**see figure 5**):

- Turn my hand palm away from me
- Flex my bicep muscle
- Squeeze my right hand toward my right shoulder.

Collar Choke from the Back

Once I have my opponent's back, I can use his collar to choke him.

This technique is known as Kata ha Jime in Japanese. I slide my hand down behind his ear (**figure 1**) and feed the collar to that hand, grabbing deep in his collar and cutting off the slack as shown in **figure 2**.

Once I have the collar pulled tight, I put the other hand behind his head, pull to the right with my right hand and push down and to the right with my right hand (**figure 3**).

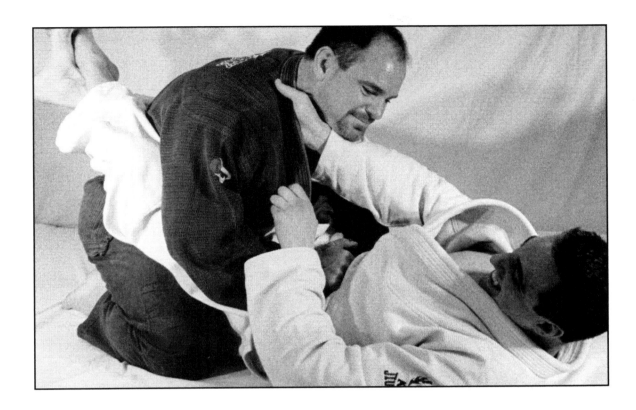

The Guard

Another one of Jiu-jitsu's trademark positions, the guard, will provide its user with the highest number of submission holds over any other position. The basic principal incorporated here is the use of four limbs (your arms and legs) against your attacker's two (arms, because the legs are required for balance). From this position, you may either turn your opponent over (sweep) or apply a variety of submission holds. Having your back against the floor gives you as the user of this position a seemingly unlimited amount of power and leverage against your opponent.

There are two basic types of guard in Brazilian Jiu-jitsu: open and closed. Any time your ankles are crossed behind your opponent's back, your guard is closed, when they are uncrossed, it is open. My suggestion to all students of Brazilian Jiu-jitsu is to practice with your guard open as much as possible.

Once your guard is open, there are many different ways to place your feet and control your opponent. Each different place ment has a name that most schools use to describe that type of open guard, but this is an advanced matter that

will be covered in greater depth in The Master Text.

The important thing to remember is to not allow your opponent to pass your guard and assume control at your side. To do this, you may use your feet to control your opponent's arms, hips and legs. Your hands may also be incorporated to assist in setting up submissions and turning your opponent over.

Your feet should be used

like hands, adding two to your controlling limbs. Your feet can be used to block punches, or stop your opponent from moving to your side (passing your guard). For this, you may place your foot in your opponent's bicep. If your opponent is moving to your left, you should place your foot in his left bicep. You may also place your foot under your opponent's left armpit and 'hook' your foot behind his left arm. As you do this, you must control his collar so he does not attack your ankle as I will illustrate in the section on leg locks. This type of guard use is commonly called "spider

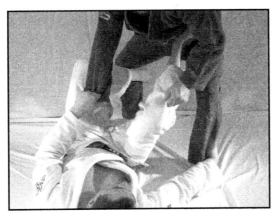

guard" and is a highly effective position from which to set up many common submissions involving your legs. Your feet may also be used to control your opponent's legs by 'hooking' under or behind them. This

will prevent your opponent from moving back or to the side. Let's say your opponent wished to move to his left; in that case, you would simply place your left foot behind his right leg, preventing him from moving that way.

Your feet may be placed in your opponent's hips as well. This action will help control the distance between you and your opponent. Remember that your legs are longer and far more powerful than your opponent's arms. This will allow you to keep an opponent who wishes to strike you at a safe distance. Control of the hips is also very important against a much heavier opponent who is trying to impose his weight upon you.

Through the combination of these foot placements, you will begin to control and off-balance your opponent. This off-balancing will present you with new opportunities to sweep and/or submit your opponent with great ease from the bottom position.

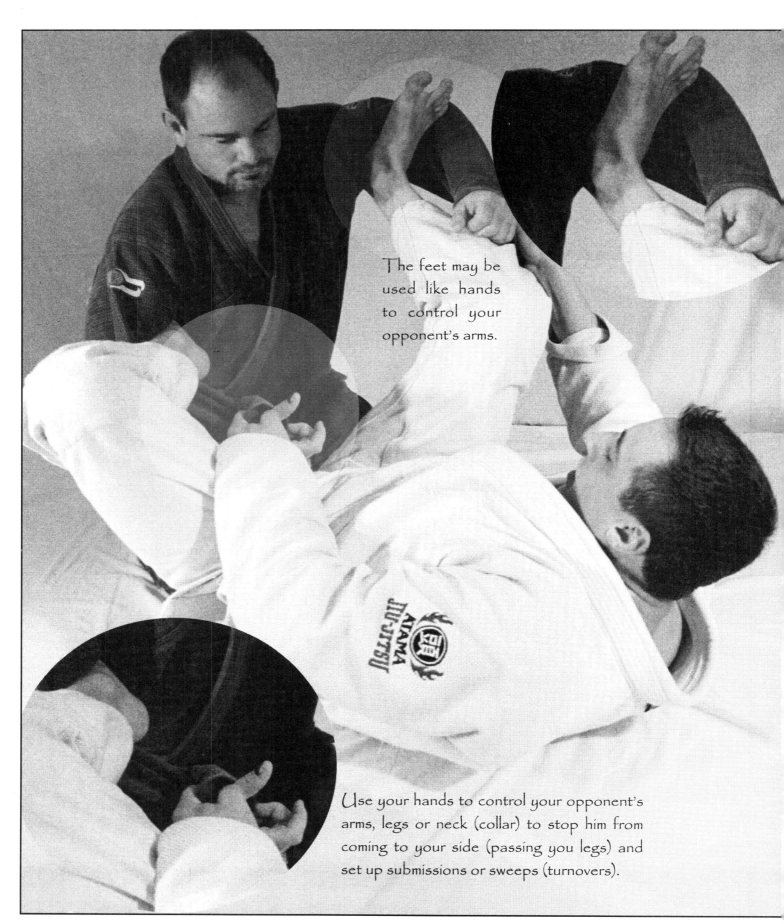

The feet may be used like hands to control your opponent's arms.

Use your hands to control your opponent's arms, legs or neck (collar) to stop him from coming to your side (passing you legs) and set up submissions or sweeps (turnovers).

Submissions from the guard

The first three submissions: 1. arm bar 2. triangle choke 3. omoplata (shoulder lock with the legs) in this section are the pillars of submission from the guard position. The reason for this is as follows: first, all three of these movements connect to each other equally. In other words, you will be able to access either one of these submissions if the first doesn't work or in the event that your opponent is making an escape attempt. The second reason for the importance placed on these movements is that they are all achieved through leverage created by your arms and legs together. This makes them very easy to apply with little use of strength. The final reason for the importance of these movements from the guard position is that they can all be performed without the use of the kimono, making them applicable in any situation. In the next few pages, I will illustrate the differences between these three moves when the kimono is not involved. The techniques without the kimono are straight from the Master Text and will give you a tiny sample of what is to come.

Brazilian Jiu-jitsu Basics

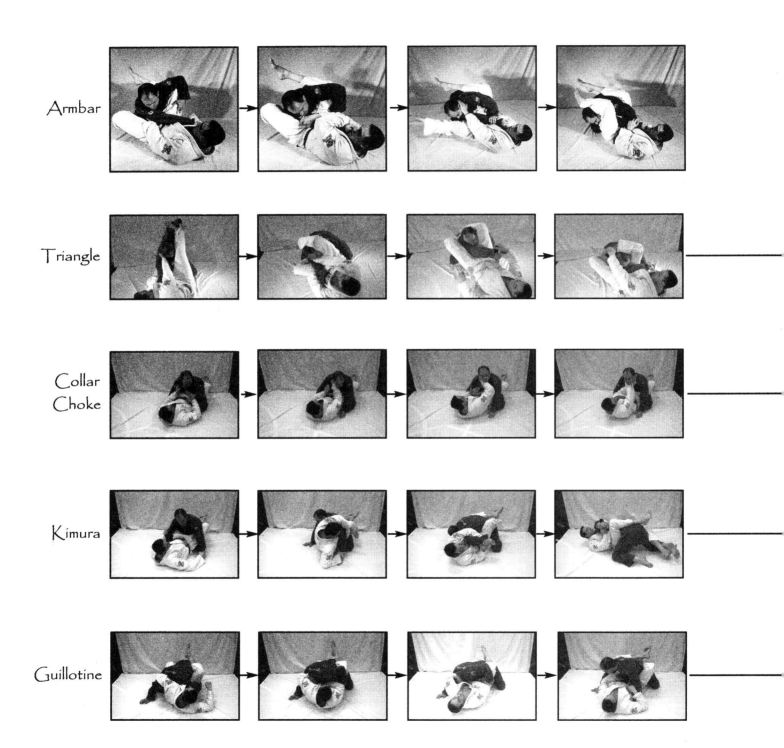

Armbar

Triangle

Collar
Choke

Kimura

Guillotine

Omoplata

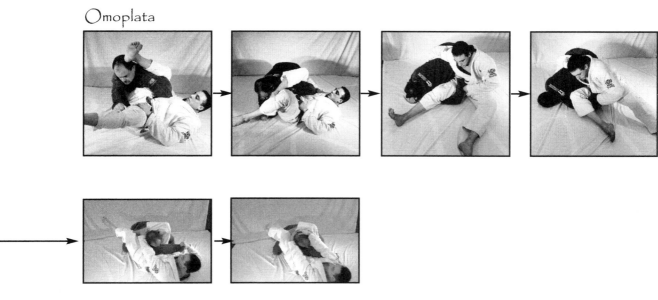

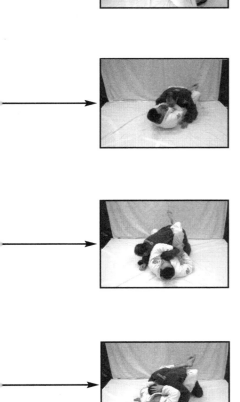

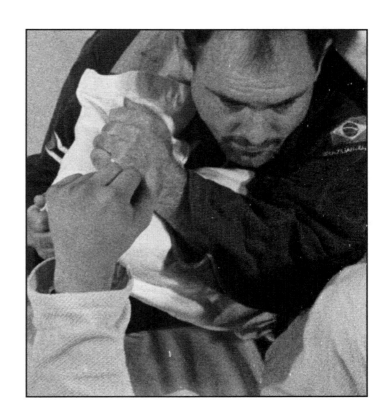

The first three submissions covered will be the armbar, the triangle and the omoplata. As I have stated, these are the pillars of submission from the guard position. What I have done to emphasize their importance is to show them **side by side** with techniques from the next book in this series that may be done without the use of the kimono, Brazilian Jiu-jitsu, The Master Text. Because there is no kimono involved, it is not sport and punching will be allowed, I have used these moves to give you a sample of what is to come without the kimono and how it will both help you with your technical game and how it will change in a No Holds Barred situation. The fundamental movements are the same with or without the kimono, but there are subtle changes that must be made, which are more drastic during these first three submissions.

The rest of the submissions illustrated in this chapter are performed with the use of the kimono. They, like the triangle choke, armbar and omoplata are essential basic submissions. I will connect some of the submissions in this chapter to other "sweeping" techniques in the next chapter, using them to set up reversals from the guard position.

Many people ask me what submissions they should learn first from the guard position as a beginner. I have organized this chapter by my opinion of an order of importance. So take one move at a time, once you learn them, you will be able to set up the sweeps in the next chapter with them, then move on to The Master Text, where you will take everything you know to the next level and sequence the submissions, combining them in order to increase their effectiveness against skilled opponents.

Arm Lock from the Guard

Here, my right leg is high over my opponent's (top) back, keeping him from posturing up. My left leg is in his hip and that knee is tight to his side.

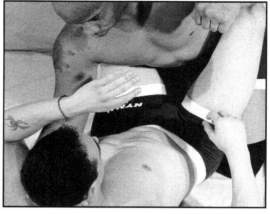

The first step is almost the same as to the left, but I am mindful of the punches to the face as I pivot to the side from the bottom to attack.

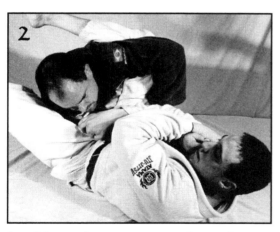

I pull his right arm to my right and pivot to the side to get the appropriate angle. If he tries to bring his right elbow to the floor, I lift my hips and pull his arm to my right, centering it on my hips.

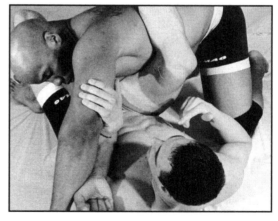

I pass his arm as shown in frame 2 so I do not get punched in the face.

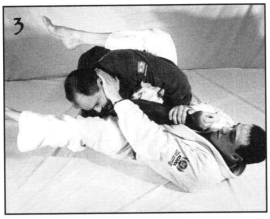

I then push his face as I continue to control his arm, making room for my left leg to go in front of it.

I then pass my leg over his face and hook his arm to set up the armbar.

To finish this lock, I squeeze my knees together, lift my hips and point my feet to the floor. his thumb should be pointed up.

Notice how I waste no time hooking the leg in case he tries to pick me up.

Triangle Choke

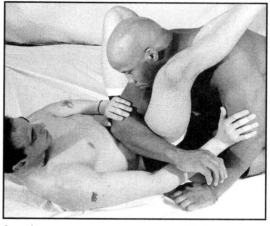

In this situation, I am pushing my opponent's bicep with my right foot to set up the triangle choke. This would also act to block his punch in a no-rules situation.

In the no - gi situation, If I am not using my foot on his bicep to set up the triangle choke, I must place my hand on his left arm as shown to protect myself from punches.

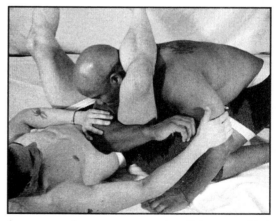

Next, I pull his arm across and pivot to the side as shown. My leg must be over the side of his neck and at the base of my opponent's skull.

In a no rules situation, I will be mindful of his free hand (left) because he may punch me as I pivot.

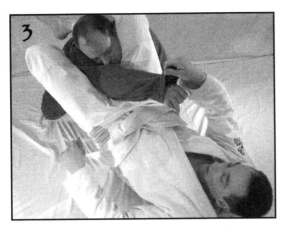

To help pull my opponent's right arm across his neck where it belongs, I will lift my hips and pull it to my right.

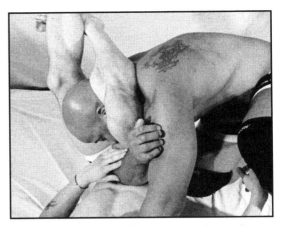

I am have locked the triangle with my legs as tightly as I can around my opponent's neck and right arm. I also remember to keep his right arm across his neck with my left hand.

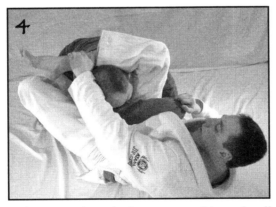

This is a detailed picture of how I will use right leg as a lever over my opponent's neck (base of the skull). Notice how I control his right arm.

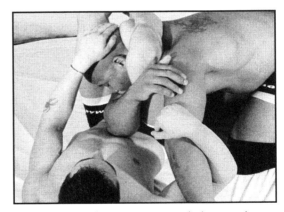

In the no-rules situation, I do not have the gi to grab onto, so I quickly triangle my legs over his neck. Notice how I am still controlling my opponent's arm. I will finish the choke by pulling down on my opponent's head, squeezing my legs and lifting my hips up.

After my right leg is completely over my opponent's neck, I will 'lock' the triangle, closing my left leg over my right as shown.

In a no-rules situation, my opponent will try to pick me up so that he can slam me to the ground to escape and hurt me.

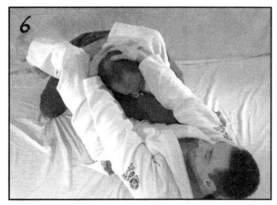

I will finish the choke by pulling down on my opponent's head, squeezing my legs and lifting my hips up

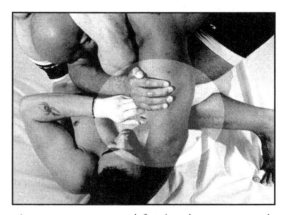

As my opponent lifts his leg to stand, I will hook under it as shown, clasping my hands together. This will attach my body to his leg and prevent him from lifting me off the floor.

Omoplata

I pivot my body to the side by grabbing his belt with my right hand and pulling myself toward his left side.

Here I push his face to he cannot get good leverage to punch.

I then kick down with my right leg and tringle it so I can sit up.

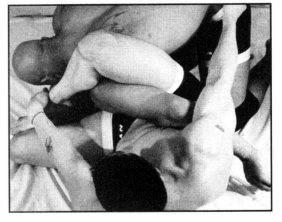

Once he is far enough away, I bring my right foot to the front of his face and grab his shorts to bring my self around.

To finish the lock, I need his shoulder pinned. I do so by kicking my right leg to the floor.

I then pull myself up to a seated position along side him.

I then turn my right leg in as shown. While securing the arm, I use my left leg to post out, making a base and sitting up toward his head.

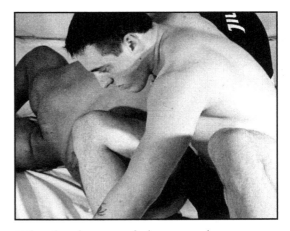

The final step of the omoplata movement from the guard is almost identical to what it would be if you had a kimono on.

Collar (scissor) Choke from the Guard

In this situation, my opponent is in my closed guard and I have decided to apply a collar choke.

Using my left hand, I open my opponent's right collar and 'feed' it to my right hand. I reach deep in my opponent's right collar with my palm up until my thumb is behind his ear (**figures 1 and 2**).

I will then grip his collar using a tight fist. My left hand will perform the same task as my right on my opponent's left collar (**figure 3**). To do this, I will lift my opponent's chin with my right forearm in order to gain access to his neck easily.

Once my opponent's chin is raised, I will place my left hand deep in my opponent's collar until it is behind his left ear as shown in **figure 4**. Once the hand is in, I will make a tight fist.

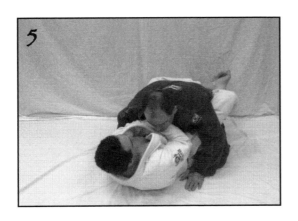

To finish the choke, I will pull down on my opponent's collar, bringing his head toward my chest (**figure 5**). To do this, I will use the muscles in my back, instead of my biceps alone.

Kimura from the Guard

In this situation, my opponent is in my guard and has placed his hands on the floor at my sides (**figure 1**). I will begin the first step of the Kimura's application by grabbing my opponent's left wrist with my right hand.

Once I grab my opponent's left wrist, I will sit up, reaching over his left tricep as shown to the left in **figure 2**.

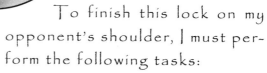

I continue to reach over my opponent's left arm with my left arm until I reach my own right wrist (**figure 3**). Once I reach my own wrist, I will grab it as shown in the circular picture below. I will keep my opponent's left arm bent at a 90 degree angle.

To finish this lock on my opponent's shoulder, I must perform the following tasks:

-Turn my opponent's left hand toward the ceiling.

-Keep my right leg over his back.

-Weave my left leg around his as shown and kick out.

Guillotine Choke from the Guard

Sometimes, I will attempt the Kimura lock and my opponent will defend by grabbing his own belt or pants as shown here to the left in **figure 1**.

If this happens, I will move to a new submission by releasing my grip on my opponent's left arm and wrapping my left arm around my opponent's neck until my left hand is under his chin (**figure 2**).

Once my left hand is under my opponent's chin, I will clasp my hands together as shown in **figure 3**.

At this point, I must remember to squeeze his neck tightly with my arms, not allowing him to pull his head out and escape. I keep my guard closed around his waist and squeeze my legs together.

To finish the choke, I not only squeeze my arms together, but I will also pull my left arm up with my right hand/arm. I will also arch back, creating downward pressure on the top of my opponent's head with my left arm as I extend my legs (**figure 4**).

Sometimes my opponent will pull his head out because I have made too much space or extended my arm too far toward the top of his head. In either case, I may use an alternate grip on his collar to assist this choke. I grab my opponent's collar deep behind his ear with my left hand (four fingers inside) as shown in **figure 5**. You must gain experience through drilling and practice in order to gauge the amount of slack you will need on his collar in order to effectively perform the rest of this movement. I then use my right hand to 'stuff' my opponent's head under my left arm as shown in **figure 6** . The rest of this movement is the same as the normal Guillotine.

Sweeps

An alternative to submitting your opponent from the guard position is reversing him. This will afford you the opportunity to apply a number of different hold down, restraining, and submission techniques from the top that may not have been available from the bottom (guard) due to an opponent's level of ability or balance. Just as in the practice of throwing from the feet, in order to sweep your opponent or turn him over from the bottom, you must first discover a weakness in his balance or create one with your knowledge of action-reaction. The following are fundamental sweeping techniques from the guard position that most instructors will require you to know before receiving your blue belt.

Using
Armbar
to Set up
Sweep

Using
Triangle
to Set up
Sweep

Standing
Sweep 1

Standing
Sweep 2

Scissors
Sweep

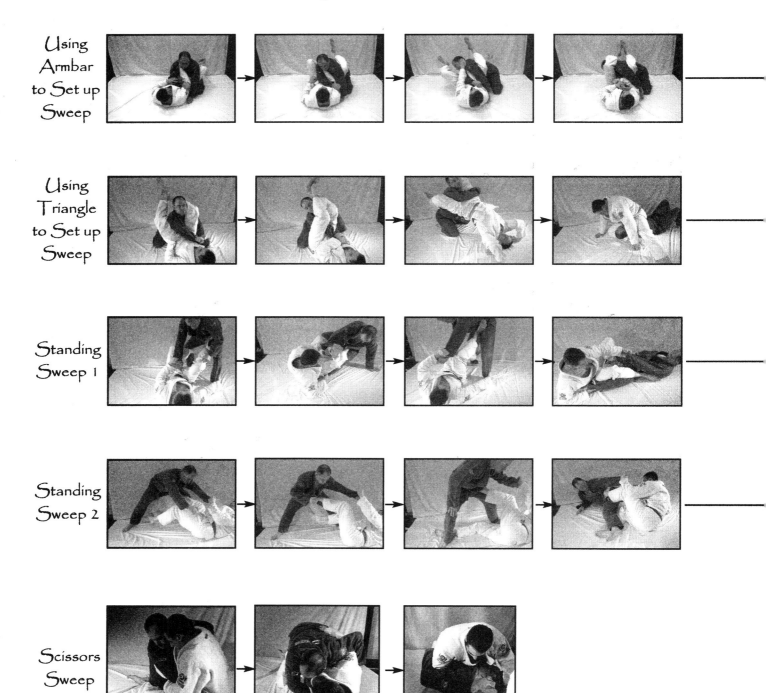

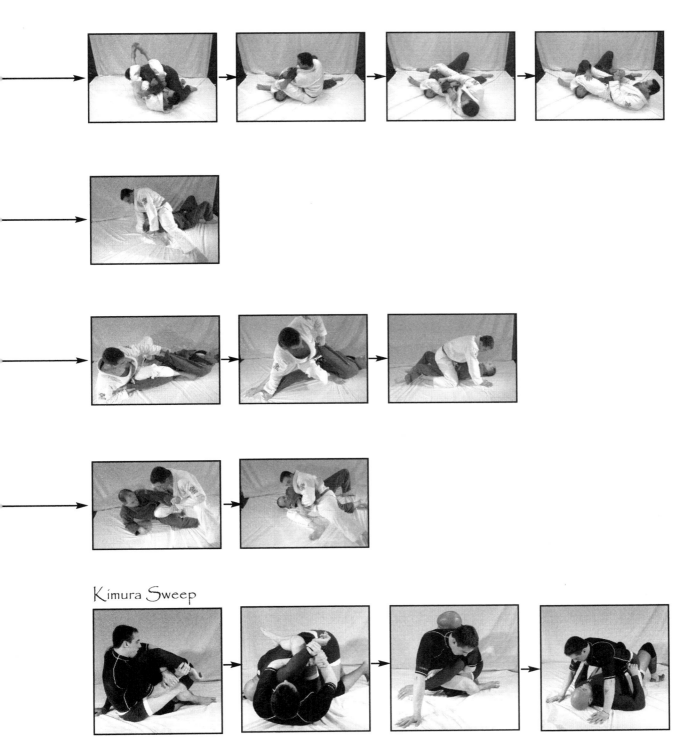

Kimura Sweep

Combination: Armlock-Sweep

In this situation, I will use a combination of the moves we have learned thus far to achieve my goal of submitting my opponent.

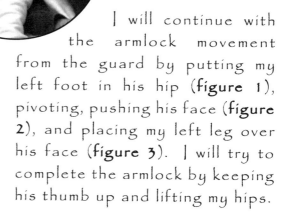

First, as shown here the circular picture to the left, I will place my hand in my opponent's collar. When he grabs my arm in order to defend himself, I will use the fact that his arm is in a perfect place to set up an armlock as an opportunity to take his arm.

I will continue with the armlock movement from the guard by putting my left foot in his hip (**figure 1**), pivoting, pushing his face (**figure 2**), and placing my left leg over his face (**figure 3**). I will try to complete the armlock by keeping his thumb up and lifting my hips.

At this point, we will continue in our sequence of movements with my opponent's defense. In order to defend, my opponent will grab his arm as shown here to the left in **figure 4**. Notice how he hooks the arm in danger (his right) with his left arm to prevent it from being extended.

Instead of using strength to pry his arm off, I will use his defense to set up my next move. I will begin by hooking my right arm under his left leg as shown in **figure 5**. I do not release my left arm from his.

I will keep my knees together and rock my body to the left, lying on my left side (**figure 6**). To assist in this process, I will lift my opponent's leg with my right arm.

Once my opponent hits the floor, I will keep my right leg over his body and my left leg over his face. This is very important! If I do not keep my left leg over his face, he will most certainly sit up and I will have to start a whole new sequence.

When he is flat on his back, he will most likely grab my pant leg as shown to the left in **figure 7**. To release his arm and complete the armbar, I will do the following things: As I continue to hold his arm tightly and close to my chest with my left arm hooked around his right, I will hold my right gi collar with my left hand. I will use my right hand to pull his left tricep, bringing his left arm toward me. As I do this, I will lie on my left side. This will make pressure on his right shoulder, causing him to release his grip (**figure 8**).

Once he releases his grip, I will lie flat on my back, keep his thumb pointed up, squeeze my knees together and lift my hips to finish the elbow lock as in **figure 9**. Sequence of moves = Choke - Armbar - Sweep - Armbar.

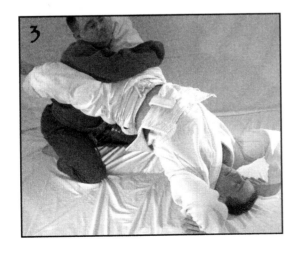

Combination: Triangle - Armbar - Triangle Sweep

In this situation, I attempt a triangle choke from the guard position. To defend, my opponent adjusts his posture properly and looks up (**figure 1**). Without the ability to pull his head down, I cannot complete the choke.

In **figure 2**, I simply place my left leg over my opponent's face in order to secure an armbar from the guard. In that situation, I may cross my ankles so that my left leg does not slip off of my opponent's face.

If my opponent bends his right arm to avoid the elbow lock, I will transfer back to the triangle choke. If his posture is still good, I will try a sweep to reverse the fight so that I am on top of him.

To sweep my opponent from the triangle position, I will do a handstand move as illustrated to the left in **figure 3**. I lift my hips up and push my body into my opponent.

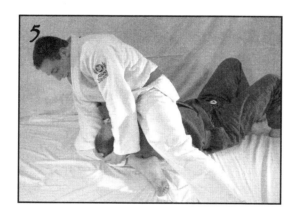

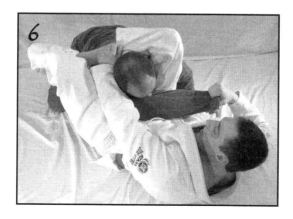

This move will drive my opponent backward until he falls flat on his back like in **figure 4**. My right leg is still folded under my opponent's neck. At this point, it is possible to finish the fight by sitting on my opponent's neck and pulling his head up toward me (**figure 5**).

If my opponent does not give in, I can roll back to my guard while pulling down on my opponent's head as shown in **figure 6**. This movement will give me an opportunity to secure the triangle choke without allowing my opponent to regain his posture though the process of rolling back to his knees.

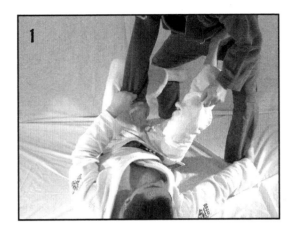

Sweeping a Standing Opponent

This method of sweeping my opponent is to be performed while he is standing in front of me (in my open guard).

Figure 1: As my opponent stands, I will place my right hand behind his left ankle and my left foot behind his right knee (calf) to control his legs and prevent him from stepping back. My right foot is placed in my opponent's hip and my left hand is controlling his right hand.

In **figure 2**, I will use my right hand and left leg to pull and my right leg to push. This push/pull action will cause my opponent to fall backward. You will notice that because I have not secured my opponent's left hand, he is able to 'post' on it, stopping me from completely reversing the position.

If I secure his left hand as shown in **figure 3**, He will have trouble creating a base in the direction I wish to sweep him.

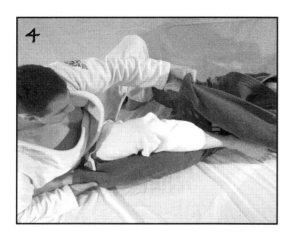

Once I sweep him to his back, I will use my left arm, which is grabbing his left arm to pull myself up onto him like in **figure 4**.

As I pull myself up, I will use my right hand on the floor behind me to not only push myself forward, but to trap his leg so he cannot back away and escape (**figure 5**).

I will bend my knees, folding my legs under myself in such a way that will allow me to achieve the mount position on my opponent as shown in **figure 6**.

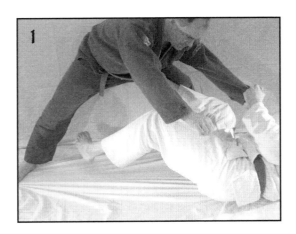

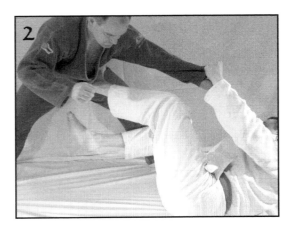

Sweep on standing opponent # 2

This is a follow-up technique to a typical defense of the last sweep shown.

In this situation, my opponent moves his right leg backward to remove my left leg from the back of his (**figure 1**). During this attempt to regain control on my opponent's part, I must react quickly and change the position of my legs in order to attack and prevent my opponent from passing my guard.

To set up the second sweep, I will switch my legs by placing my left foot on my opponent's hip in place of my right foot as shown in **figure 2**.

Once my placement is complete, I will move my left heel to the back of my opponent's right leg and lie on my right side (**figure 3**). I am still maintaining control of my opponent's left leg and arm.

To sweep my opponent to his back, I will push with my left leg and I pull with my right hand. At the same time, I will sweep my opponent's right leg by kicking my right leg behind his right leg and toward me.

As my opponent falls back, just like the previous sweep, I will pull myself up using my left hand.

In this situation, due to the angle, it will be very difficult for me to achieve the mount position. Instead, I will move to side control by driving my right knee over his right leg and sliding through to his side on my right side to a modified kesa gatame hold.

Scissor Legs Sweep

In this situation, my right shin is across his belly with my right knee pointing to the left (**figure 1**). My left leg is on the ground blocking his right leg as shown. I sit up, holding his arms as shown. My right hand reaches under his left armpit and grabs his belt. I then use my weight to roll back, bringing his body on top of my hips like in **figure 2**.

I then make a 'scissor' move with my legs, kicking my right leg to the left and my left to the right, turning him to my left, landing in a mount position as shown in **figure 3**.

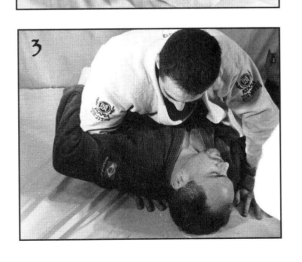

Kimura Sweep

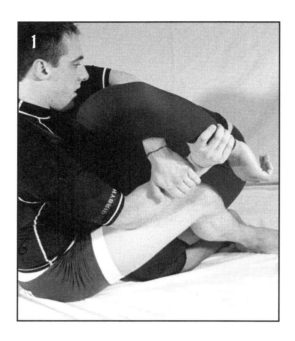

In this situation, I will begin to perform the Kimura lock from the guard just as shown in the previous chapter.

I have taken the opportunity to give you a sample of a technique from The Master Text to show how Jiu-jitsu can be done without a kimono. This technique is from the Submission Grappling chapter of the Master Text, which deals with the sportive practice of Jiu-jitsu without a kimono.

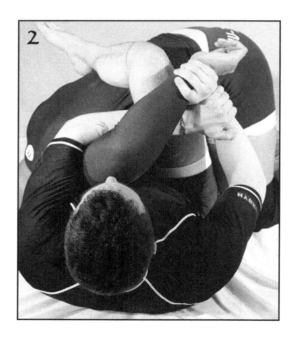

Here, you can see the details of the kimura lock from the guard very clearly (**figures 1 and 2**). My right hand is controlling my opponent's left wrist, pushing it toward his head and my left hand grabs my right wrist to keep my opponent's left arm bent at the appropriate angle.

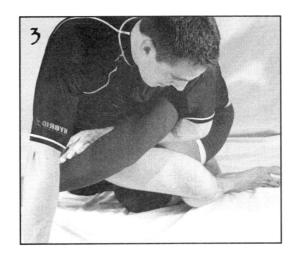

In this situation, my opponent resists the kimura lock. To begin the kimura sweep (sometimes called the belly sweep) , I will place my left arm over my opponent's left arm as shown here to the left. I will reach all the way over my opponent's arm until my left hand touches his.

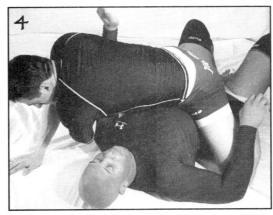

I will place my right hand on the floor and use my arm to lift my hips off the floor, driving my hips into my opponent (**figure 3**).

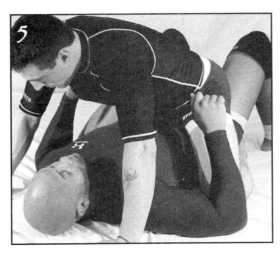

I drive my hips forward and pull his arm into my belly, sweeping him over and to my right side (onto his left) into the mount position as shown in **figures 4 and 5**.

Escapes

The best method of escape is prevention. It is like getting sick; the best way to avoid contracting an illness is to live a healthy lifestyle that consists of sleep, diet and exercise. Once you find yourself in an uncompromising position, you will be working against your opponent's positional dominance and increased leverage. This is why it is important to understand the principles of attack described previously in this book. By understanding the attack, you will be able to anticipate what your opponent is about to attempt. It is inevitable, however that as a beginner you will find yourself trapped under a larger and/or more skilled opponent. Here is a list of escaping techniques that newcomers to the art of Brazilian Jiu-jitsu are required to know.

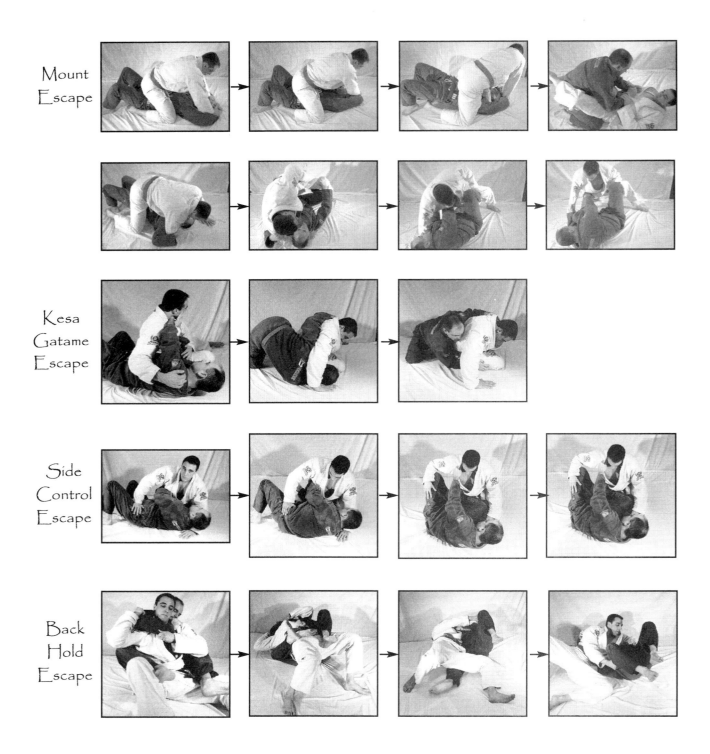

Mount Escape

Kesa Gatame Escape

Side Control Escape

Back Hold Escape

The Escaping Movement

Sometimes, called the Shrimping move or the Snake move, the Escaping movement is one of the single most important movements you will ever learn during your Jiu-jitsu practice. It's applications will eventually tie into many areas of guard work and escaping, so much that your ability to perform this move will determine your level of proficiency later at higher levels of training.

First (**figures 1 and 2**), start flat on your back and lift your his (bridge) high in the air. Once your hips are completely off the floor, shift to your side as shown is **figure 3**.

Note: This movement is sometimes shown without bridging your hips first. By bridging your hips, space is created between you and your opponent, who may be trying to hold you down.

Once you shift to your side, push off, extending your legs while bending forward, touching your toes (**figure 4**).

Repeat on both sides, moving yourself backward across the floor.

Once you are comfortable with this movement, try taking it one step higher by moving to your knees.

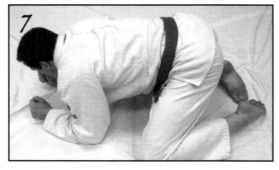

You will do this by performing the escaping move almost the same way as before. Instead of touching your toes, You will bring your right leg under your left until you are facing the floor on all fours (**figures 5 through 7**).

Mount escape using Escaping Movement

In this situation, my partner (bottom) will use his escaping movement to escape the mount position.

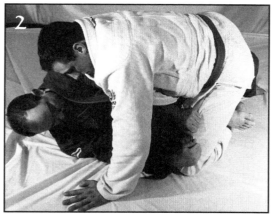

In this example, he pushes on my left leg with his right hand and escapes his hips, causing my legs to spread open (**figure 1 and 2**).

Once he has enough space, he brings his right leg under mine (**figure 3**), then repeats the process on the other side.

Escape from the Mount Position (Upa)

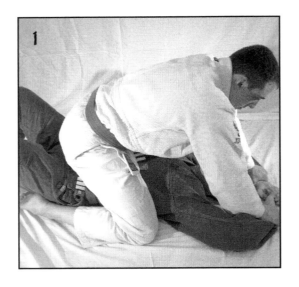

In this situation, my partner will use his escaping movement to the knees to get me off of his chest. You will notice that in **figure 1**, I am on top of my partner and pinning both of his wrists to the floor.

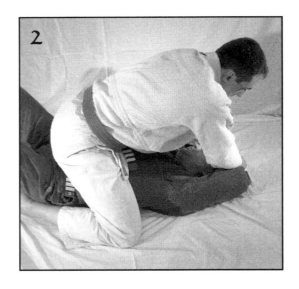

To get out, he will slide his hand to the opposite side that he will be rolling, this will pull my hands away from the direction I will be falling and limit my ability to post my right hand out and create a base with which to stop the roll (**figure 2**).

My opponent bridges his hips high in the air as shown in **figure 3**. If I remove my hand from his wrist, he will hold my right arm with his left arm and pull it toward him like in **figure 4**.

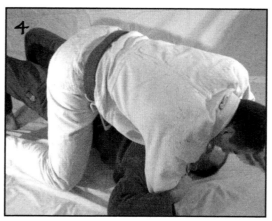

I may post my right leg out and create a base with it, If this happens, my opponent will try to trap it (my right leg) with his left leg. But this is often very difficult to achieve in a realistic situation.

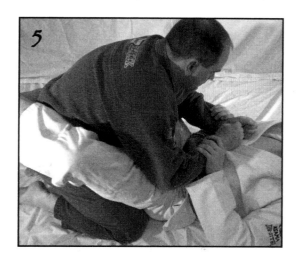

My opponent will use his escaping move to the knees until he rolls all the way up, reversing the position and landing in my guard (**figure 5**).

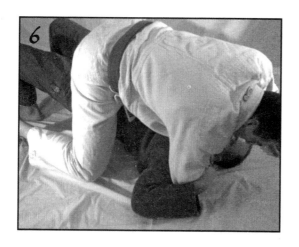

In this situation, my opponent is bridging to get me off of him as he did before (**figure 6**), but as you can see, I have posted out with my right leg to make space and defend.

The fact that I have posted my leg out has created a considerable amount of space. With this space, my opponent will escape his leg under mine, using the first escaping movement in this section as shown in **figure 7**.

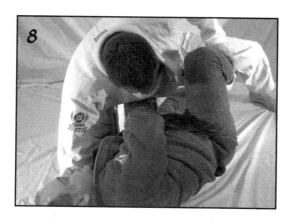

He will keep his hips up in the air until he can push my leg or hip and slide his leg under my raised body like in **figure 8**.

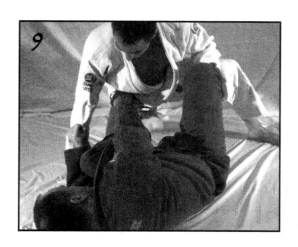

He will escape his legs by pushing on my hips on both sides until he has regained his guard (**figures 9 and 10**).

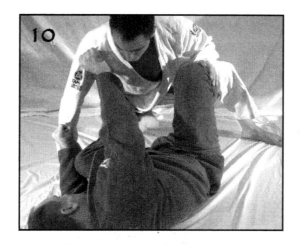

A lot of instructional text will show these two moves alone, but that is not the most effective way to perform them. Even at the most basic levels, you should use the upa movement to set up the escaping movement in order to remove yourself from the mount position.

Escape from Side Control

In **figure 1**, I am leaving space between my opponent and I to allow him to demonstrate the side control escape.

My opponent moves his left hand under my right arm and places both of his hands on my hips (**figure 2**).

My partner pushes on my hips with both hands (**figure 2**) and escapes his hips using his escaping movement away from me.

He then slides his leg in between us (**figure 3**) until he has the space to get his guard back.

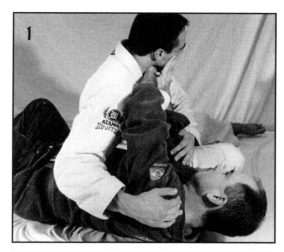

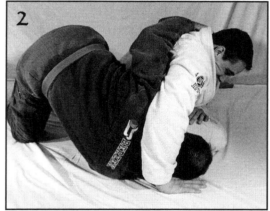

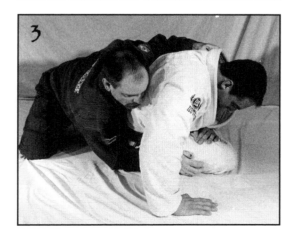

Escape from Kesa Gatame

In this situation, I have trapped my opponent in a modified kesa gatame hold.

To escape, my opponent pushes my face like in **figure 1** and makes some space with his hips, using his escaping move. He brings his right elbow (not shown) to the floor between us and pushes on my hip.

My opponent escapes his hips (moves them away - **figure 2**) to the left, moving away from me. He escapes to his knees until he has both knees on the floor. At this point he will be in an advantageous position (**figure 3**).

Escape from Back Mount

In this situation, my opponent has achieved back mount and is trying to apply the mata leo choke.

If your opponent has your back and begins to choke, pull his arm down hard. Here, my opponent has my back. I grab his right arm with both hands like in **figure 1**.

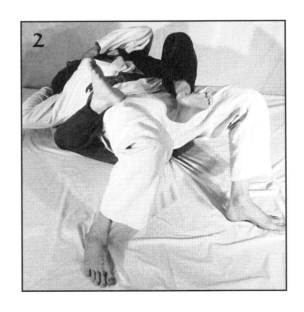

In **figure 2**, I bridge up on my toes, lifting my hips off the floor and start to move in the direction of the arm I am grabbing. I then slide myself to the side, sitting on his leg.

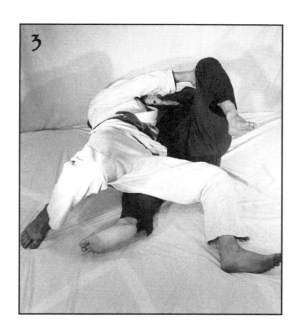

I slide myself to the side, sitting on his leg. You will notice that as I do so, I am controlling my opponent's leg with my right hand as in **figure 3**. The purpose for doing this is so my opponent cannot place his leg over my belly and achieve the mount position. When I am almost out, I switch my base and pass the leg to end up in side control.

I will move my right hand to my opponent's hip in order to control him and completely hold him down. My left hand will now control his hip on the opposite side of his waist.

I will now assume a reverse kesa gatame position along side my opponent in order to hold him down before I decide my next attack. Notice how my left leg runs parallel to his body (**figure 4**) and my right leg is posted out to provide me with a base and prevent from being rolled onto my back.

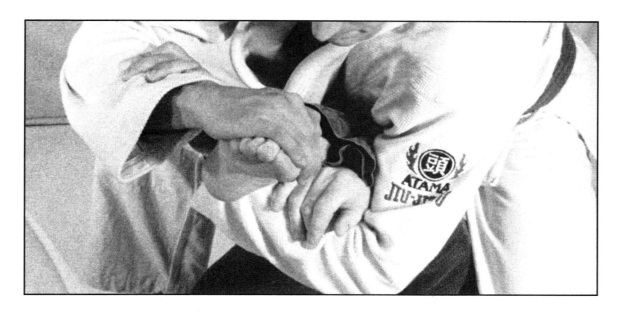

Leg Locks

For reasons of safety and other philosophical complexities, leg lock techniques in Brazilian Jiu-jitsu are usually a secondary method of attack. It is, however important to learn and understand them. You will probably find that responsible instructors will not allow you to perform these techniques as a beginner during regular free sparring practice. There are two fundamental reasons for this: the first is because accidents do happen in every sport. If you are allowed to perform leg locks at full speed and resistance, it is inevitable that you or your partner will eventually make a mistake and injure that area. If an injury to the leg occurs, unlike an injury to the arm, the recipient will be extremely disabled and may not be able to attend work or other important life callings and typical duties. The second reason is that the nature of the nervous system in the are of the foot is such that the recipient of the lock will often times not feel pain before damage to the ligaments occurs. A student will eventually gain the experience and level of maturity that will trigger a willingness to submit to this type of lock, but in the beginning of your Jiu-jitsu practice, you will not yet have this foresight.

Ankle Lock

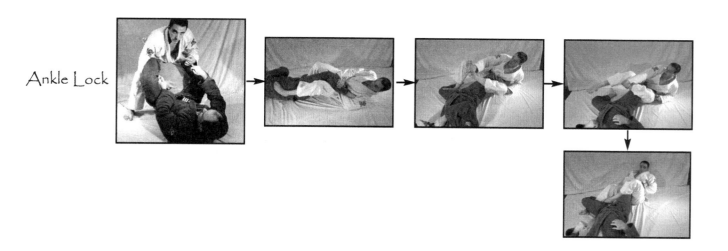

Escape

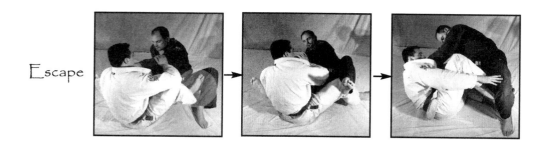

Knee Bar

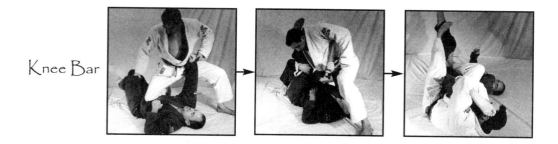

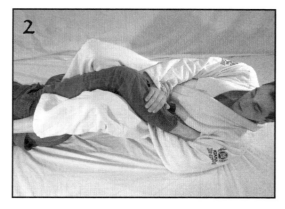

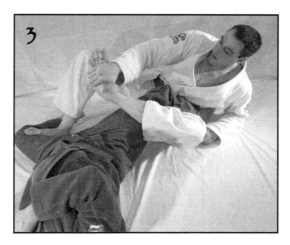

Ankle Lock

During the next few pages, I will demonstrate a lock that will affect your opponent's achilles tendon. This lock is dangerous and should be performed with the greatest possible caution.

Because it is the easiest position from which to explain this lock, I will start IN my opponent's guard. I must emphasize at this point that when you are in the guard, you should at this level, be developing the skills to pass it.
I stand in my opponent's guard when he has his foot under my armpit as shown (**figure 1**).

My arm wraps around his ankle and I will fall to my back with one leg between his legs and the other foot on his hip/stomach to stop him from sitting up and mounting me. In **figure 2**, I am showing a method of squeezing the knees together in order to secure the lock.

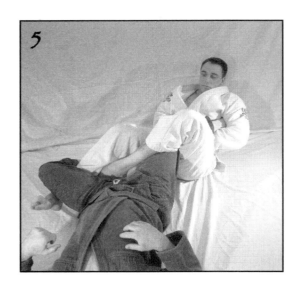

My left hand is under his right ankle with my forearm touching the lowest part of my opponent's ankle. I place my right hand on his shin and my left hand on my right wrist.

To finish the lock this way (**figure 2**, previous page), I arch back and lift my wrists up by turning my hand around my own wrist.

The next method of securing the lock is by trapping my opponent's leg with my own.

To do this, I push my opponent's left leg away with my right leg (**figure 3**, previous page). I then make a "triangle" with my legs as shown, with my left ankle under my right leg like in **figure 4**.

I may then place my right foot under my opponent's left leg to prevent him from rolling in order to escape the lock (**figure 5**).

The and position and method of finishing the lock is the same as illustrated in figure two in the previous page.

Escape from Ankle Lock

As you will recall from the previous page, the element that was preventing my opponent's escape was my right foot on his left leg (**figure 1**).

To escape, my opponent must move his left leg over my right leg as shown in **figure 2**. He will then grab my collar in order to pull himself onto me and improve his position.

As my opponent sits up to achieve the mount position, I push his hip or leg with my right hand and move my knee toward my chest as shown in **figure 3**, blocking him from sitting on my with my right shin.

Knee Bar

In **figure 1**, I have a dominant position on my opponent. I am pulling up on his arm with hopes to secure an armlock, but it seems as if he knows what I am about to do.

Instead of performing a predictable movement, I will attempt a knee bar. This is a lock that will affect my opponent's knee joint.

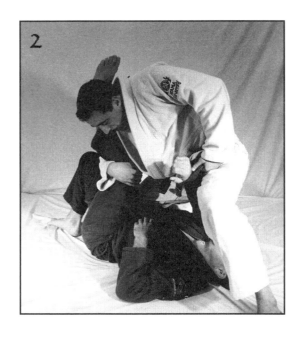

From knee on belly, I move to grab the outside leg (my opponent's left) with my right hand. Once I begin my move, stepping over my opponent's head, I hug his knee and get my body close to it as shown in **figure 2**. As I spin around him, I keep my weight low.

I move around my opponent until I am sitting on his chest facing away from him as shown here in **figure 3**. My opponent's foot is on my right shoulder and I secure his leg by hugging it at the ankle.

Once the leg is secure, I will fall to my side on the floor, keeping the knee-cap by my belly. The movement and position is similar to the armbar (elbow lock), with his knee acting as the elbow joint.

Once I land, I make sure his knee is facing my belly and his toes are pointing toward my face. I stretch his legs out with by pushing on his as shown in **figure 4** and squeeze my knees together around his leg. To finish the lock, I extend my hips forward and pull on his ankle.

157

Epilogue

Mastery of the techniques in this book could take a lifetime; therefore it is not necessary to do so before moving on to the next book, _Brazilian Jiu-jitsu, The Master Text_. My advice is to reach a level of basic proficiency and comfort with a high percentage of the movements in this book. After doing so you may begin to add, link and sequence new techniques from The Master Text in order to expand your physical vocabulary.

This book is also available on DVD, which includes special bonus features and extra techniques. It is available only at www.jiu-jitsu.net, where you may also ask your technical questions in the sites discussion forums.

Good luck for now, as you acquire skills, you will no longer need it.

- Aranha

Biography of the Author

Gene Simco was born into a family of artists, musicians and educators. His father was a schoolteacher and a classically trained organist. His mother, a teacher educated in Europe, exposed him to the arts at an early age. His father began teaching him to play the piano at the age of five, which inspired a passion for music

that would follow him throughout his adolescent life. By the age of eleven, he had become proficient in more than one instrument and appeared on his first recording. His mother nurtured a natural ability to draw and paint that led him to major in the visual arts throughout high school.

Early in Gene's adolescence, doctors discovered he had a form of dyslexia that was causing him problems with his academic studies. At the age of nine, an optometrist recommended the study of Karate to improve his hand-eye coordination. Because of this, his physical abilities began to flourish, bringing to the surface his natural aptitude for athletics. When he was twelve, his physical education teacher encouraged his parents to enroll him in track and field, citing instances of his exceptional running times. But fate had other plans for Gene, moving him upstate from his home in Westchester County, New York, to Poughkeepsie at the age of fourteen. While residing in Poughkeepsie, he pursued a musical career and postponed his martial arts training. During that time, he wrote over fifty songs and performed on numerous recordings, funding some of them on his own with his natural entrepreneurial spirit. Graduating from high school at the age of eighteen as an art major, he continued his musical career by playing in bands. But something was missing: the life of a musician is not always the path of health and fitness.

By the age of nineteen, his lifestyle as a musician had made him frail, unhealthy, and weak. To create balance, Gene returned to his martial arts training by enrolling himself in both a Jeet Kune Do school and a school of ancient Japanese martial arts that specialized in the practice of Jiu-jitsu, Aiki-jitsu and modern Judo. Sometimes attending two classes per day, he began a rigorous strength-training program and committed himself to better health. It was at the school of Japanese Jiu-jitsu that he met with friends who had extensive backgrounds in Greco-Roman Wrestling and Western Boxing. After reaching a pinnacle with his Jeet Kune Do instructor, he devoted his time fully to the training of grappling arts. Gene eventually earned the respect of his peers and instructors and was asked to join the black belts during their training sessions. Here, he was introduced to the secrets of Japanese martial arts passed down through generations of warriors. At this time, he was also training at Brazilian Jiu-jitsu academies all over the United States. With the information learned there, he began to improve his grappling skill and depth of understanding in the art of Jiu-jitsu. During the course of his Jiu-jitsu training in many schools of the art, he faced many opponents in no-holds-barred matches.

His genetic inclination as an educator and entrepreneurial instinct soon drove him to establish the NYMAG academy in Poughkeepsie, N.Y., where he began teaching the art of Jiu-jitsu as taught to him by his first master. As his study of Brazilian Jiu-jitsu continued, his pursuit of the world's finest training led him to California where he was awarded a Blue Belt (in Brazilian Jiu-jitsu) by Joe Moreira. Because of his understanding of Jiu-jitsu, it was not long before Marcio Simas awarded him a Purple Belt while training at his school in Florida. It was the achievement of this rank and love of the Brazilian form that inspired Gene to strip himself of his black belt in an act of humility that showed him to be a true Martial Artist. From that point on, he wore his rank in Brazilian Jiu-jitsu proudly and began teaching under a new flag. He spent nearly the next four years of his training at this rank, gaining experience on the mat in both sportive and non-sportive matches. During this time, his reputation grew, causing his academy to flourish; his team's percentage of wins averaged eighty-ninety percent. He eventually made a great name for himself as a Jiu-jitsu instructor, leading many fighters to victory in both grappling tournaments and no-holds-barred fights.

As business improved, the prospect of traveling extensively to train became less likely and, consequently, he employed many leading instructors to teach at NYMAG, including a Brazilian Black Belt who taught a weekly class. It was through this training that Gene had the opportunity to travel to Brazil and gain some of his most valuable experience, leading him toward the rank of Brown Belt. During this time, he founded what became the largest resource for Jiu-jitsu on the Internet, www.jiu-jitsu.net, and became the first to offer online illustrated techniques and the first to author multiple books on the subject of Brazilian Jiu-jitsu. After testing his technique in both Sport and Vale Tudo matches, he decided to pursue his career as an educator. In 2002, he was awarded his Brown Belt by Michael Jen.

After writing six books on Brazilian Jiu-jitsu and publishing several instructional DVDs, Gene continues his dedication to the arts and the noble profession of teaching. He is President of NYMAG, Ltd., a company that owns the NYMAG Academy of Brazilian Jiu-jitsu (where he teaches) and NYMAG Films. He also publishes a line of books and an online magazine, JIU-JITSU.NET, as well as running an assortment of enterprises in the media industry. You can contact Gene at his website: www.GeneSimco.com.